The Model Shipbuilding Handbook

THE MODEL SHIPBUILDING HANDBOOK

BRICK PRICE

Chilton Book Company | Radnor, Pennsylvania

Copyright © 1983 by Brick Price
All Rights Reserved
Published in Radnor, Pennsylvania 19089, by Chilton Book Company
Manufactured in the United States of America

Library of Congress Cataloging in Publication Data
Price, Brick.
     The model shipbuilding handbook
     Includes index.
     1. Ship models—Amateurs' manuals. I. Title.
VM298.P74   1983   623.8'201   83-70781
ISBN 0-8019-7218-3
ISBN 0-8019-7219-1 (pbk.)

1 2 3 4 5 6 7 8 9 0   2 1 0 9 8 7 6 5 4 3

To my
best friends
(still),
Laura and
Eamonn Price

Acknowledgments
Laura Price; the Staff of Brick Price
Movie Miniatures, Inc.; Darryl Anka, Troy Hughes,
Felicia Greene, Craig Coleman and Bosco of
Century Models in Anaheim, California;
Nilso Rios, Steve Amos, Fred Hill, Michael Mulvey
and (who could forget) Bruce MacRae.

CONTENTS

The Model Shipbuilding Handbook

INTRODUCTION

Model shipbuilding is a fascinating hobby which encompasses a broad range of skills and interests. Whenever we hear of a ship modeler we tend to think of someone who builds large sailing ships, such as the *Cutty Sark* or *Constitution*. However, there are also those who like to build models of smaller vessels, such as a tugboat, or a diorama where the ship is but a part of a much larger image. The intent of this book is to appeal to all of these modelers, as well as the newcomer who knows nothing of ships.

I hope to take you from the very basics of ship modeling, through to more sophisticated techniques. Part of the fun of model shipbuilding is to meet and beat the many challenges which crop up during construction. Most of the procedures described here are as simple to follow as a cookbook recipe. If you don't try any shortcuts, you should have excellent results the first time through. As your skills develop, you can find new and easier ways to do things.

One thing I find interesting is the distaste that seasoned modelers in various clubs have toward plastic models. Part of this is surely the desire to produce an authentic, valuable model, but part of it may be some outmoded ideas regarding other materials. I agree that if I were to scratchbuild a model of the *Cutty Sark*, I would rather make it out of wood then strip styrene. But if I simply wanted a nicely detailed model of the same ship for my den, I would surely consider modifying and super-detailing either the excellent Monogram or Revell plastic models. I know how to fool

FIG. 1–1 Most modelers prefer the large sailing ships because of the intricate rigging.

the most practiced eye into believing that the plastic hull is weather-beaten timbers with barnacles, so the wood is not as important.

Another curiosity I discovered about most seasoned ship modelers is their abhorrence of weathering. Part of my joy of viewing real ships is noting the rich textures of heavily aged wood, rusty

FIG. 1–2 Revell's Constitu-tion has been a consistent bestseller since its introduc-tion more than 25 years ago.

metal, soot on the exhaust, etc. You can almost tell the history of a ship by the scars it bears. I can sympathize with someone who, after spending hundreds of hours building a gorgeous model, has to deliberately tarnish the finish. It must feel akin to taking a hammer to a new car. However, I personally wouldn't feel that the model was complete until it looked as though it had spent some time in the water. The chapters on superdetailing and weathering cover the techniques you'll need to create an outstanding model.

The information in this book is the combined knowledge of myself, modelers who work for me at Brick Price's Movie Miniatures Inc., and members of various shipbuilding clubs. Some of the procedures are recent innovations that we have developed to cope with the pressures of building quality, realistic models given precious little time or money. One of the primary considerations and the ultimate goal we face daily is that the model must appear absolutely real on film. If we fail in that, the illusion of reality with the rest of the film may be lost. Perhaps it's this training and background which makes me appreciate the aging process so much.

I've been building models professionally for more than twenty years, and yet I continue to discover or develop new ideas on a daily basis. Every new job brings with it a new set of problems which must be solved. The ideas thus generated become a part of our regular repertoire. I also find that I can learn a lot from people who work for me even though they may be relatively new to the business. The point is, don't assume that you know everything and stagnate. Much of this book may seem old hat if you are experienced, but parts of it will surely seem brand new. Keep an open mind to learning and you'll be rewarded with exceptional models to display and enjoy.

Once you've developed basic skills, you may want to advance to kitbashing plastic kits or a full-blown craftsman wood kit. Kitbashing (cross-kitting) is an interesting area because it allows you to build complicated-looking models out of inexpensive kits, while you might otherwise have to scratchbuild the same thing. I have described several examples of this, including a how-to section showing the creation of a fishing trawler from a Revell tugboat kit.

Don't be afraid to tackle one of the larger kits. In talking to several builders of professional-looking models, they said that their first ship was one costing hundreds of dollars. The kits are very thorough and you can rest easy knowing that spare parts are available in case you make a grievous mistake. Don't allow yourself to be overwhelmed with the apparent complexity of a model. Each of the assembly steps is spelled out in great detail in the better craft kits.

Scale

If you want your collection to be more interesting and consistent, try to build everything to the same scale. This can be useful since you'll be able to compare prototype differences at a glance. To increase interest, a display or diorama should have recognizable elements of scale in it—a human figure is the simplest thing to

FIG. 1–3   Figures are a good scale reference because people can instantly relate to their size.

FIG. 1–4   Within a diorama, try to keep all objects to the same scale. These models are all HO (1/86) scale.

relate to for most people. In a diorama, it's essential to make everything in one scale, unless you intend to create the illusion of depth with forced perspective. In this case, you'll want smaller objects in the background, which won't upstage the foreground model in detail.

Ships tend to be scaled smaller than other types of models because of their size. Even a 1/100-scale model of a large ship will be three feet long! The range of common scales is from 1/48 to 1/700. The first scale is for smaller vessels such as sailboats, while the latter is reserved for such waterline-scale models as aircraft carriers. You may find reference on kits for scales which are very similar but not exact. For example; 1/48 (0 scale) is an American scale because it is based upon ¼ inch equals a foot; 1/50 is a metric scale derived from tenths of an inch. These scales are so close that parts can be interchanged without any difficulty. This is also true with other similar scales, such as 1/72 and 1/86, except that the spread is great enough here that you're really taking a chance of the differences being noticed.

TOOLS

Tools are essential for model-building whether you build kits or start from scratch. The most important thing you could ever do is to buy good quality tools and learn how to use them properly. A simple tool kit can be put together for less than ten dollars and should consist of a modeler's knife, half-round file, sandpaper, glue, and bottled paints. From this simple beginning, the avid modeler or professional can literally spend thousands of dollars.

While it is possible to build a sizeable collection of tools at minimal cost, it can prove to be penny wise and pound foolish. Buy quality tools one at a time, as you can afford them, rather than purchase a large number of "bargain" tools initially. Modeling is a precise art form, and you cannot do precise work with sloppy tools. Stocking your workbench may require the purchase of some inexpensive tools at first, but these should be replaced with better quality items as soon as possible.

Poorly maintained tools will do poor work and are the sign of a poor craftsman. If you take pride in your tools as well as your work, you will find the hobby much more enjoyable. Keep a clean, orderly work area which is well-ventilated and well-lit. Keep your tools safe and organized, preferably in a machinist's chest. Knives should be sharp, lightly oiled after use, and protected in cardboard sheaths. Steel tools are prone to rusting; a quick wipe with an oily rag will keep shears, pliers, and others looking and working like new. Don't dump tools into a drawer without protection; files

FIG. 2–1   This well-lit work
area looks out on San Diego
Bay.

which rub together will soon have dull cutting edges. Make a
compartmented box or a rack to keep tools safe and readily available.

Modeler's knife

A modeler's knife can take a lot of punishment because the blades
are replaceable. You can use a knife on thin metal flash, as well
as for cutting all kinds of wood and cardboard. The best type is
the surgeon's scalpel. The blades are incredibly sharp and last far
longer than ordinary modeler's knife blades. The shape of the flat
handle and the keen cutting edge allow for far better control.
However, they are hard to obtain; they're expensive; and you can
lop off a finger tip in a heartbeat.

When cutting with a knife, observe how the blade cuts in each
kind of operation and you will soon have control for very accurate
work. Try shaving thin layers from wood, and cutting card or thin

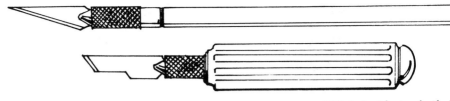

FIG. 2–2 The top knife is the most common type in general use and is fitted with a no. 11 blade. The heavier knife is useful for carving or gouging wood.

wood by drawing the tip of the knife along a line many times. Always test the knife on a scrap piece first, so you will know exactly how the material will behave *before* you make crucial cuts.

The most commonly used knife is an X-Acto with a No. 11 blade, available in almost any art or hobby shop. There are many other blade shapes as well, and a larger handle for wood-carving blades. Don't press too hard with the knife; it cuts almost as fast with light pressure, and the light cut will be more accurate and safer.

Files

The variety of files is endless. The knife-edge, half-round, triangular, square, and rat-tail are most useful. Your best bet is to have a collection of 6-inch files in varying shapes and cuts, plus a complete set of Swiss-pattern needle files. A collet-type handle (available from X-Acto) should be used with the latter for improved convenience.

A file card is a useful device for taking care of files. It is a flat, paddle-shaped piece of wood with a multitude of stiff wire bristles, and is used to "scrub" your files, moving it parallel to the teeth to remove clogging.

While files are often thought of as being virtually indestructible, when they rub together, or are tossed into a drawer or box

FIG. 2–3 A variety of files of different shapes and cuts are essential for shipbuilding.

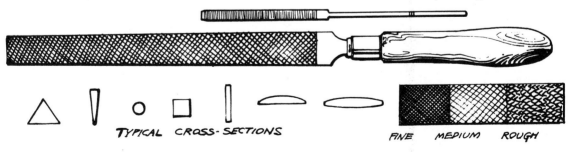

TYPICAL CROSS-SECTIONS

FINE MEDIUM ROUGH

FIG. 2–4 A file card is used to keep files clean and sharp.

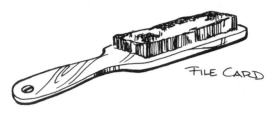

FILE CARD

with other tools, their cutting edges may be dulled. A dull file clogs easily, tears the work surface, and won't produce a good finish. Wrap them in heavy fabric for best protection.

Mill file

A smooth single-cut mill file about 6 inches long is very handy for removing flash from die-cast metal and molded plastic parts.

FIG. 2–5 Top, improper filing. Bottom, the proper technique for holding a mill file. Using the correct technique while filing will assure a better looking model.

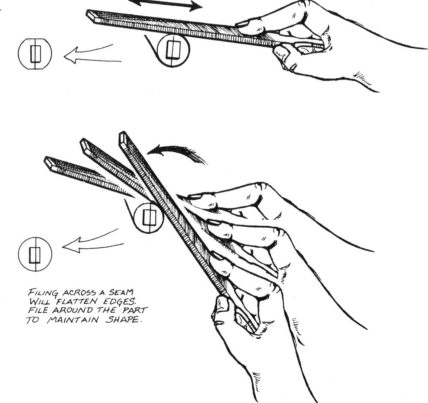

FILING ACROSS A SEAM WILL FLATTEN EDGES. FILE AROUND THE PART TO MAINTAIN SHAPE.

THE MODEL SHIPBUILDING HANDBOOK

It's also useful for making any surface smooth and flat. A file cuts by scraping minute shavings from the surface of the work. Always lift it on the back stroke so you don't wear flat tops on the file teeth. If the file makes a low buzzing noise and cuts a waffle pattern in the work, clamp the work more securely and file from another direction.

Solder and other soft materials will clog the teeth of a file. Apply a little graphite lubricant to avoid this. Remove the clogged material with the end of a soft stick of wood.

Mill files are flat but other useful shapes include triangular or round files. Be sure to buy good handles for your files; the handles may save you from a painful accident and will allow better control.

Needle files

These come in a variety of shapes, and are sometimes called jeweler's files. They are useful for shaping small parts and getting into tight areas which might be inaccessible to a larger file. The teeth on this type are very fine and closely spaced, allowing for minute amounts of material to be removed at a time.

The best way to buy these initially is in a set with all of the different shapes. You may find a preference for one shape over any other. I usually use the half-round file for all of my modeling.

There are also very fine files, as small as a pencil lead in diameter, but these are fragile and delicate. You may want to delay buying a set of these until you are more experienced in modeling and can pinpoint your needs.

Sandpaper

Sandpaper is sold in sheets and in various grades of roughness (known as the grit). The finest grit you will probably need is #600, which is used for final sanding of finished pieces. When used with rubbing alcohol or water, #600 can smooth out uneven paint jobs prior to buffing. The rougher grits, #50 to 280, are used for rough shaping of wood or putty. The medium-fine grits, #320 to 400, are useful for sanding a surface just prior to painting. You may find that it's better to rough up a normally smooth surface with #320 so that paint can adhere better.

A useful tool you can make in a few minutes is a sanding block. Contrary to what you may think, the block should be rigid and hard. The block will give you a smooth, even surface rather

FIG. 2–6 Some tools, such as this sanding block, can be homemade and will make your work easier and and better. Block sanding is the only way to assure smooth, straight lines.

A BLOCK OF SOFT WOOD MAKES A GOOD SANDER.

than simply evening out depressions. You can shape a piece of pine to suit your needs and glue a piece of sandpaper in place. As an alternative, several companies make aluminum sanding blocks in various shapes.

A handy, often overlooked, item for your tool kit is an ordinary emery board, which can be bought at any cosmetics counter. One side has rough-grit paper while the other side is fine. The backing is fairly rigid as well, and they are cheap enough to be disposable.

Clamps and vises

Like any other tool, clamps and vises come in a wide variety of shapes and sizes. Ship modelers, more than others, need a broad

FIG. 2–7 Small clamps are indispensible for holding small parts during painting or while glue sets. This type uses rubberbands for tension.

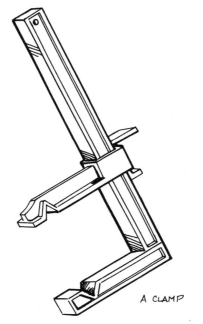

A CLAMP

THE MODEL SHIPBUILDING HANDBOOK

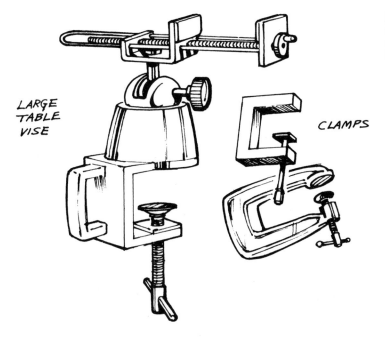

LARGE
TABLE
VISE

CLAMPS

FIG. 2–8 A swivel vise is used for holding objects at odd angles while working on them.

selection of several types. Cheaply made vises can't be expected to be useful. The jaws usually tweak out of alignment and the gear drive becomes sloppy. Don't skimp. You can get small vises, but be sure they are of good quality and suit your needs. Check the vise carefully: make sure the jaws fit squarely and that the guides are smooth and true.

A small vise with a swivel head (Dremel or Pana-Vise) can be as useful as hands growing out of your forehead. A large machinist's vise is good for drilling, filing, or other shaping work. The larger vise can be used to hold delicate items, but be careful not to crush them by overtightening the jaws.

Clamps are available in aluminum for use as soldering heat-sinks, to draw heat away from delicate parts. There are also large, powerful spring clamps which can exert too much pressure. Probably the most useful clamps are made out of ordinary clothespins. You can buy these by the dozens and shape them with Dip-It plastic coating to suit specific jobs. Wood clamps are also useful when you don't want them to rob heat while soldering. Just be careful that they don't catch fire.

FIG. 2–9 A vise can be used to clamp pieces for gluing, if you do not over-tighten it.

FIG. 2–10 Clothespins are simple and inexpensive clamps. They can also be easily modified to fit a specific application.

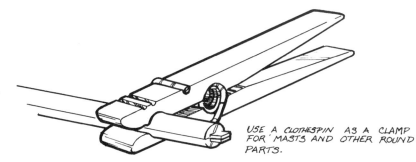

USE A CLOTHESPIN AS A CLAMP FOR MASTS AND OTHER ROUND PARTS.

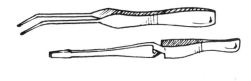

FIG. 2–11 *Tweezers come in a variety of styles, all useful. The type shown are different in that the top one is squeezed to hold a part while the bottom one is squeezed to release.*

Tweezers and forceps

Tweezers are absolutely essential for fine modeling and handling small parts. The better ones are the surgical grade. Most well-stocked hobby shops can get them if you ask. Even the best ones are cheap, so get several types and sizes.

Another useful surgical tool is forceps: a cross between locking pliers and tweezers. They can pick up a small part, then lock to hold the piece firmly. I find these useful for holding small parts while I'm shaping or painting them. Again, most hobby shops can order them, but you may be forced to order from a surgical supply house.

Pin vise

The pin vise is really not a vise at all, but rather a collet with a handle, something like a drill chuck. It can be used to hold small round parts while working on them, or other tools, such as drill bits. They also hold taps for threading small holes.

You'll need pin vises of various sizes. The best type contains two double-ended collets giving a total of four sizes in one convenient tool. The handle can be removed to hold long pieces of wire or rod which can pass through the stem.

FIG. 2–12 *A pin vise can be used for tiny drill bits or to hold small parts.*

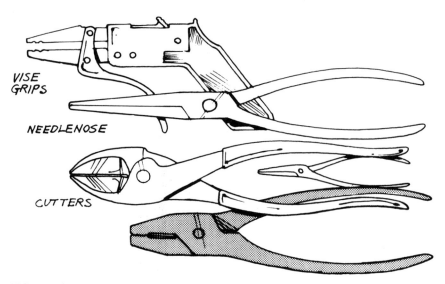

VISE GRIPS

NEEDLENOSE

CUTTERS

FIG. 2–13. The pliers
shown are the most useful
types you'll likely need.
Vise grips are self locking.

Pliers

Pliers come in an infinite variety of sizes and shapes. The "jeweler's pattern" pliers with a 4-inch needlenose will be most useful. The larger, 6- to 8-inch, needlenose is good for holding larger pieces or for bending wire and small parts. Most of these contain a cutting edge for wire, metal or plastic sprue. Be sure to buy the case-hardened type and never use them for cutting piano wire or they will be nicked and ruined.

Special pliers are available for bending wire and can be used for creating the eyes and hooks so common in a ship model. Electrician's pliers or vise grips should be used on very large objects. The vise grips lock and will hold virtually anything.

Shears

Technically, scissors are shears and can be used as such for cloth, thin plastic, or thin, soft sheet metal, but they will dull easily. A complete toolbox would include duck-billed tin snips for rough metal work, electrician's scissors for cutting sheet metal, and good household shears for plastics and paper. The best all-purpose shears I've found to date are made by Dixon of West Germany and are widely available in most hobby or craft shops. These have short, thin, easily maneuvered blades, and loopless handles. They seem capable of cutting almost anything without a whimper or apparent damage and cause only minimal distortion of the material being cut.

Hammers

A conventional claw hammer really doesn't serve any purpose for the average model shipbuilder, but you will probably have one around the house anyway should the need arise. A small ball-peen hammer is good for shaping metals and driving brads home. A small jeweler's hammer can be used for driving nails and other normal chores. A rubber mallet may be needed for gentle prodding.

Screwdrivers

Screwdrivers are common tools which are often taken for granted and misused. Don't ever use one for prying or chiseling—there are special tools for those tasks. Keep the screwdriver tip sharp by occasional grinding. Be careful that you don't get the tip too hot, or the metal will lose its temper and become too soft to be

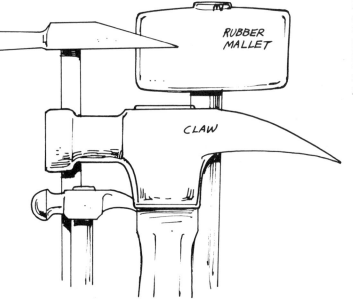

RUBBER MALLET

CLAW

FIG. 2–14 *Hammers are seldom used in miniature work but are still needed for construction of cases or bases. The rubber mallet can be used in place of a hammer when the object is fragile.*

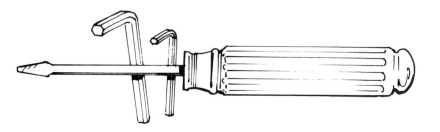

FIG. 2–15 *You will need screwdrivers with both flat and Phillips heads. A set of small jeweler's screwdrivers and Allen wrenches are also useful.*

useful. Always select a screwdriver with a tip as wide as the screw, or it will slip causing damage to the screw and work piece.

Your tool kit should include all of the common, standard sizes of flat and Phillips types, as well as jeweler's screwdrivers. The latter usually come in a plastic case for storage.

Saws

Saws are generally used for roughing out work from wood, metal, or plastic. Here again, there are a variety of saws you'll likely need for shipbuilding. A coping saw features interchangeable blades which are available in several tooth configurations for cutting anything from wood to metal. Be sure that the saw you choose has a deep U-shaped throat for better maneuverability. You also want to be sure that the blade can be tightened until it rings when struck. A loose blade will break in an instant. When inserting the blade, be sure that it cuts when drawn toward you, the opposite of all other saws.

Sears sells a small hacksaw they call a "hobby saw" which is good for rough cutting. You'll also need a pointed-blade saber

FIG. 2–16 *The three saws illustrated are a must for model ship building. The coping saw can make fine, intricate cuts not possible with any other saw.*

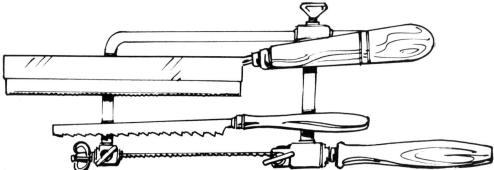

THE MODEL SHIPBUILDING HANDBOOK

18

saw to make inside cuts after drilling a starting hole. A stiff-back Zona saw or X-Acto razor saw is used for making fine, straight cuts through most materials.

Power tools

Power drill
A good quality ¼-inch drill can be useful in a variety of ways. The most obvious, of course, is in drilling holes up to one inch in diameter. For most operations, you will probably want a drill press attachment stand, which will allow you to do fairly precise work. Ship modelers will find that a simple wood and brass turning lathe can be made using a simple drill stand.

A good hand drill can be expensive, but cheaper units will allow the bit to wobble and create egg-shaped or tapered holes. I find the cordless drills to be very handy around my shop.

Drill bits
The size and type of bits you'll want to buy will depend on the type of modeling. Fractional sizes from ¹⁄₁₆ through ¼ inch are useful for mounting masts or drilling out cannon barrels. Smaller numbered bits, 60 through 80, are very fine and are useful for mounting belaying pins or creating rope mounting holes. Either

FIG. 2–17 A large electric drill is useful for producing mounting holes for masts, support rods etc.

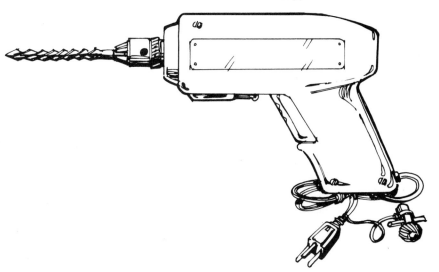

FIG. 2–18 A good quality drill can serve double-duty as a lathe if set up with a stand.

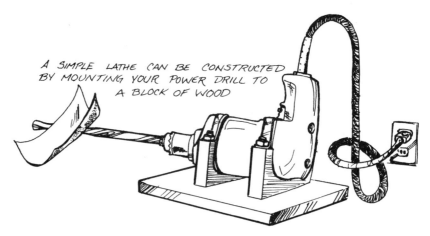

A SIMPLE LATHE CAN BE CONSTRUCTED BY MOUNTING YOUR POWER DRILL TO A BLOCK OF WOOD

FIG. 2–19 Subminiature drill bits and tools are often available in convenient sets.

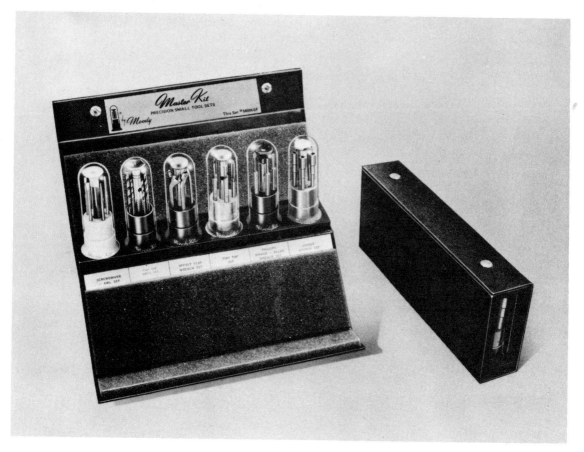

group can be purchased as a set in a handy case which will protect the drills and let you know the sizes at a glance.

Nearly 90 percent of all modeling work can be done with the following drill sizes: No. 42, 52, 56, 60, 65, 70, 75, and 76. If you need a $\frac{1}{16}$-inch drill, use a No. 52 instead; it is only .001 inch larger.

You'll find that the finished model will look neater and be sturdier if you are careful to use the proper size drill for a given job. For instance, measure a rod with micrometers prior to installation to determine the exact size. The drill you'll want to use will be within .001 plus or minus from this. In other words, use a .063 drill to clear a .062 rod.

Drills can also be used to create pilot holes for fasteners such as nails, brads or screws. Any fastener has to force itself through the object it's fastening and displace material. This usually causes the work piece to split. A simple solution is to drill a hole which is .005 inch smaller. The drill removes material and clears a path for the fastener. By drilling the pilot hole undersized, the fastener can still do its job properly.

Drill bits won't break as easily as you might expect if they are handled properly. I have a complete set of numbered drills (very tiny) which are a year old and in daily commercial work. The secret to long drill bit life is patience and care. If the flutes (sides) of a drill clog up with debris, or if the bit binds, it will snap instantly. Run the bit into beeswax before each use. The wax acts as a lubricant to prevent binding and overheating. It also keeps debris from collecting as rapidly. Back the bit out of the workpiece occasionally to allow chips to fall away. Mount the workpiece firmly and use a sensitive drill press whenever possible. A pin vise can be used to hold the small drill in a chuck which otherwise might be too big.

High-speed tungsten bits will last much longer than carbon twist drills but are considerably more expensive. They are necessary, though, if you use a power tool rather than drilling by hand.

Flex-shaft

Most modelers seem to gravitate towards the Dremel-style motor hand tools rather than a flex-shaft. Perhaps it's because of the cost, but I don't know of anyone who would prefer that type of set-up over a flex-shaft once both types have been used. The flex-shaft (Foredom is a good one) allows for a larger, stronger motor which operates cooler and lasts longer, while providing plenty of power. Since the motor is not integral with the tool, you have a lighter work head with more precise control. Now that I've used one of these, I would feel lost without it. You must get a variety of sanding, grinding and cutting bits plus a good foot control for optimum use.

Jeweler's lathe

A good quality jeweler's lathe is fast and precise for creating parts such as cannon barrels, belaying pins, brass lamps, stair spindles, or other objects with cylindrical cross-section. Other methods may be substituted but not as well. The Austrian-made Unimat (EMCO) costs nearly $300 for the basic unit and accessories will add another $200+ to the total. Sears makes a unit which is less expensive, but it is not as durable or accurate.

Power saws

I've often said that it takes big tools to build small models and it's true. The little table saws you might buy in a hobby shop are almost useless compared to even the worst large table saw. Rockwell makes an excellent unit which can be used for stripping wood and shaping pieces. A veneer blade has very fine teeth and produces cuts so fine that they need little sanding to be finished.

Another large shop tool which will win a place in your heart is the band saw. Most brands use a continuous steel blade of various teeth types or a sandpaper strip for contour sanding. The finer teeth are useful for cutting soft steel, acrylic and brass. The coarser teeth will make quick work of large pieces of wood. One of the main advantages of a band saw is its ability to cut unusual free-hand curves almost as tight as the width of the blade. This scroll-cutting is most useful in hull shaping.

Compressor

The compressor isn't a power tool in the strictest sense, but is electrical and placed here for that reason. The most obvious use of a compressor, with tank, is to supply a constant source of air at any preset pressure for use in airbrush painting. A larger, ½-horsepower compressor with separate tank is better than a single stage (single cylinder) hobby-type compressor because the flow of air is smooth. Small units tend to spit air out in pulsed bursts, which can ruin a good paint job. I have a two-stage compressor which is intended for hospital use and it's fantastic because the

FIG. 2–20 *A large compressor is expensive, but for top-quality work it is almost a necessity.*

air flow is instantaneous and smooth. As an added bonus, it is quiet enough so that it won't disturb the neighbors. I have this unit hooked up to a foot treadle which allows me to turn it on and off at will.

Soldering tools

Too often people will shy away from soldering simply because they're afraid of the unknown. It is the only satisfactory method of joining metal parts. The techniques are really simple and are outlined later in this book. If you've never tried soldering before, practice on a piece of scrap first until you've learned the technique.

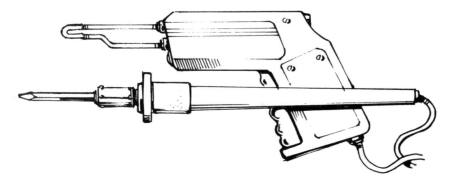

FIG. 2–21 *Soldering guns or pencils are good for electrical work or joining brass parts. A pencil can also be used for wood burning or engraving wood.*

You should get a small soldering pencil, a large iron, a small torch and a soldering gun. The small pencil is good for very tiny pieces and wiring, or for wood burning. The large iron will yield enough heat for joining sheets of brass or brass turnings such as gun barrels. The gun is a convenience item because it heats up quickly and has a fairly small tip.

Soldering with a torch is quicker and simpler than with an iron because the area to be joined is heated very quickly. This rapid heating also means that there is less chance for adjacent parts to be loosened as heat is transferred. Exercise extreme caution at all times when using or storing a torch and tanks. If you're using large tanks, chain them in place and check the valves for leaks with soapy water. Small tanks are better for most of your needs and are available from surgical supply houses.

Note: Acetylene can "pool" in areas and cause serious damage if ignited. Wear goggles at all times and be sure to turn the oxygen on last and off first to avoid an explosion.

Layout and design equipment

Every modeling job requires some planning and design or layout. Even a simple straight saw cut must be defined, or the tool can wander and ruin the job. The most basic layout tool is a 6-inch flexible steel ruler about ½ inch wide, graduated to thirty-seconds on one edge, sixty-fourths on the other and tenths and millimeters on the back side. You will probably want a ruler for whatever scale you're building. This way, direct measurements can be made off blueprints, which will eliminate the need for confusing calculations. A carpenter's square or a machinist's square is good

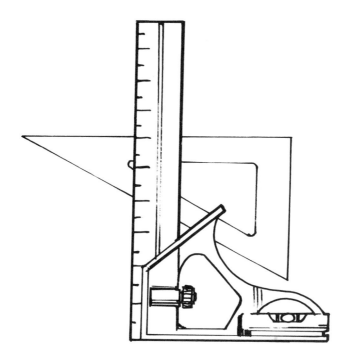

for making sure parts are aligned and true. On a ship model this is particularly important.

Considerable time and effort can be saved by using locking dividers to transfer dimensions from drawings to the workpiece. You can even double or triple the scale of drawings easily by stepping off the dimensions (walking the divider legs). Thus 1/48-scale drawings can be used to directly model a 1/24 object.

A sharp pencil with medium (no. 2) lead is satisfactory for layout work on wood but a scribe is needed for plastic or metal. Machinist's dye (such as Dyekem or even a blue marker) will make layout work easier on metal or plastic.

The centers of holes to be drilled must first be located with a center punch so the drill does not wander. The depression of a punch keeps the drill exactly on center.

Most art supply stores have an excellent selection of templates ranging from simple triangles to French curves and ellipses. Most templates are inexpensive enough that you'll probably want several. A circle template is also handy for measuring dowel, but be aware that allowances are made for pencil width, so the template hole may be slightly larger than indicated. The flexible French

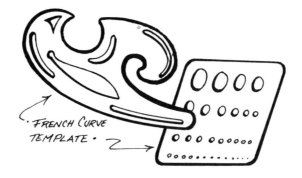

FIG. 2–23 A French curve is necessary when first laying out the contours of the hull or deck. A circle can outline gun ports or mast holes.

FRENCH CURVE TEMPLATE

curve is well suited for joining known points along the outline of something such as a hull. Never attempt to draw a compound curve free-hand.

Brushes

Watercolor brushes have the right qualities for most model work. A good brush can lay paint on your models almost as evenly as

FIG. 2–24 Taking proper care of brushes will assure that they will always be in good shape when needed.

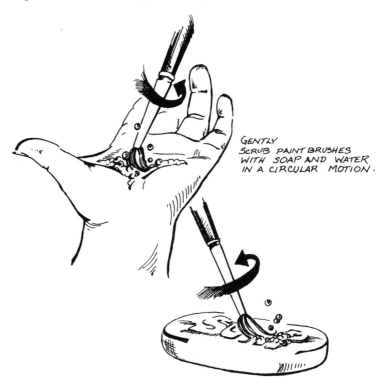

GENTLY SCRUB PAINT BRUSHES WITH SOAP AND WATER IN A CIRCULAR MOTION.

PROPER WAY TO
STORE PAINTBRUSHES.

IF YOU LEAVE THEM
IN A JAR LIKE
THIS.

THEY WILL LOOK
LIKE THIS.

FIG. 2–25 *Always store brushes upright and dry.*

a spray can, and it will keep a fine point so you can use it for both broad strokes and fine lettering. Size #3 holds about the right amount of paint for most major model work. For painting larger areas get a #5 brush.

Clean the brush thoroughly so paint doesn't dry near the base of the hairs, causing them to break off later and spoil your work. Use thinner recommended for the paint just used (i.e. enamel thinner). The brush can be used for any kind of paint, as long as you clean it thoroughly each time. The most often spoiled tool is the paint brush, but careful cleaning will add years to the life of a good brush. Store so the point is up and protected.

Airbrush

An airbrush isn't essential, but it can dramatically improve the quality of your work. Models require that everything on them be miniaturized to the same scale. A large brush with heavy marks will give the scale away instantly. The airbrush applies a smooth, fine coat of paint.

A good compressor with a large storage tank is handy to power the airbrush, but you can get by with a smaller compressor or even

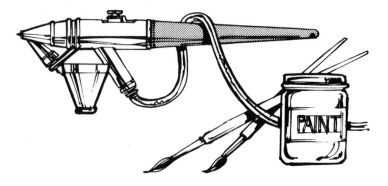

FIG. 2–26 An airbrush can produce the most professional painted finish. Detail painting should be done with a brush.

an aerosol can like the type sold by Paasche or Binks. Paasche makes one of the best airbrushes, but a Binks or Thayer and Chandler will do a good job.

Taps and dies

Many assembly jobs require the use of nuts and/or bolts and tapping and threading. Tapping is the operation of making threads inside holes; threading is making external threads on a rod or similar part. A useful range of taps includes 00-90, 0-80, 2-56, and 4-40. The first numbers of the reference number (00, 0, 2, 4) indicate the diameter while the second numbers refer to the number of threads per inch. Taps can be held in a regular tap handle or a pin-vise.

In addition to each tap, you'll need two drills. One is called the clearance drill, while the other is the tap drill. The tap drill produces the proper size hole for tapping. The clearance drill creates a hole large enough for the screw to go through. Tables of tap-versus-drill size are available but it is just as easy to select the drill which will just pass through the hole in a nut of the same size as the tap, and use this as the tap drill.

To use a tap, drill the hole with the tap drill and remove any accumulation of chips. Insert the tap, keeping it at right angles to the surface, and begin to turn it very carefully. After several turns, remove the tap and blow or shake the chips out of the hole. Reinsert the tap, make several more turns, and again remove. Continue to do this until the hole is fully threaded. Like most cutting tools, a tap is very brittle and the slightest excess pressure will break it, so proceed very cautiously. Never apply too much torque to the tap wrench or pin-vise.

Threading is performed with threading dies held in a die holder. Threading is accomplished much the same as tapping, except that you are working on rod, tubing, or square stock filed down to approximate size. The end of the piece to be threaded must be tapered slightly, to give the die a chance to grip. Use lubricants when tapping or threading to prevent binding. When tapping or threading plastic, special care must be taken to avoid heating the work, since the tap or die will seize. It's best to use soap as a lubricant, or work under running water, if possible.

Safety

While on the subject of tools, we should mention that safety is a requisite to professional modeling. Always keep the work area neat and clean. Knives can be hidden in junk and cause serious

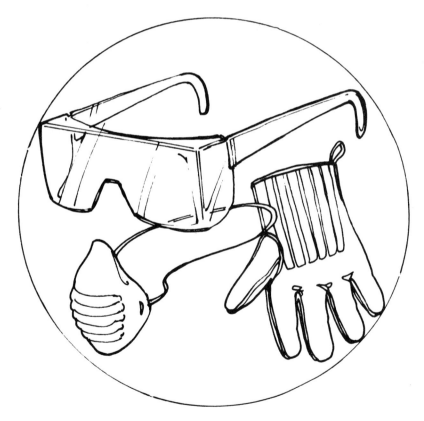

FIG. 2–27 Always use the appropriate protective gear when working with toxic materials or power tools.

injury. Many a modeler has nearly lost a finger to an X-Acto knife, which can be as sharp as a surgeon's scalpel.

The toxicity of various types of adhesive and paint should not be taken lightly. Some industrial liquid cements can cause nausea, headaches, and serious physical damage in the worst cases. Paints, such as lacquer, contain solvents which can also be hazardous. Work in a well-ventilated area unless the product is labeled as being non-toxic.

Always wear safety glasses when using power tools. Small chips of styrene can be as painful and as dangerous as metal. Your eyes are your second most useful modeling tools after your hands, so take good care of them. If any type of glue, paint, or solvent should enter the eye, call a doctor immediately and rinse the eye with copious amounts of clear, cool water.

Lighting is critical for proper vision and safety. Use a draftsperson's fluorescent desk light or industrial lamp for even lighting.

Always keep clear of power tools and never wear loose clothing or jewelry while working.

These few tips should keep your hobby healthy and fun.

MATERIALS

Your choice of material at the beginning of a project can ultimately affect the way the model appears when it's completed. It can also affect your feelings toward the model as work progresses. A poor choice of material, or cheap products, can make your work very difficult and unenjoyable. Cheap products can even cause the finished model to cost more while making it look worse, since you may have to redo much of the work.

A good example of this would be the use of balsa wood throughout your model rather than a good bass or gelutung. The balsa will fuzz and splinter while you're working with it and will require additional sealing when finished. The model will feel lighter and will lose that good quality heft. If that isn't enough, the texture and grain will be grossly out of scale. Is it worth the savings of two or three dollars now to have a poor quality model later? Most people will agree that it isn't.

The following sections list various favored buildings materials and adhesives to use with them. It won't do you any good to make fancy parts unless you can stick them all together in the end.

Wood

Wood is the material of choice for the traditional ship model-builder. The best types are bass, clear pine, gelutung, walnut, cherry, teak, and oak. The woods you'll need will vary with the

3

FIG. 3–1 This model uses
a variety of materials, from
wood to plastic.

application. Each of the construction sections of this book will
tell you what is best to use for a given application.

All of the woods mentioned here have very fine grain and are
relatively hard. Some woods are chosen for their carving characteristics. Gelutung is an excellent wood for carving. Clear pine
and bass are perfect for planking and spindle turning. Oak and
walnut are best for bases, although I've met some modelers who
use strips for planking because of the beautiful grain patterns.

Plastics

Styrene is the plastic preferred by most kit manufacturers because
of its ability to reproduce fine detail and its low cost. The best
type is a virgin white styrene, because it is pliable and easy to
shape or glue. Clear styrene for some reason is brittle and crazes
easily. Clear styrene will shatter like glass if you try to score and

snap it like other plastics. Pigments generally weaken styrene and change the characteristics. Black, for instance, has a high degree of carbon making it very soft and gummy. Be careful when gluing any pigmented plastic.

Resin or fiberglass require mixing chemicals to create hard parts. Resin, either polyester or epoxy, can be used for molding parts as outlined later in this book. There are new polyurethanes on the market which can reproduce parts from molds with less hassle, but these are generally only available in bulk lots.

Fiberglass is a cloth which has been soaked in resin to form a sheet or shell. An excellent-quality, hollow-hull model, which will be virtually indestructible, can be made using fiberglass, but this is a messy and smelly process. It can also be hazardous and expensive, making it more suitable for the professional than the home modeler.

Metals

Many different metals exist which are useful to modelers. Most parts of a ship model are made out of wood, but you will still need some type of metal for gun barrels, anchors, exhaust stacks, etc.

Brass
Brass can be readily machined and soldered together to form model parts of beauty and substance. Most commercially available parts are made either of brass or white metal.

Aluminum
Aluminum is easy to work with and can be polished to resemble silver, but it can't be welded or soldered by the hobbyist. In fact, most glues and paints don't work well either. If you must make something out of this material, hold the pieces together with fasteners such as screws.

Steel
Steel has very limited applications except for making brackets, mounts or the like. It can be silver-soldered or welded.

Adhesives

There is no one material that is suitable for all of the assembly jobs that crop up in the construction of a model. Some of the available adhesives, with emphasis on what to expect of each of them, are described below.

Acetate cements

Common acetate cements are Ambroid, Duco, and other "model airplane" or "household" cements. Most of them are very fast drying. This type of cement is made by dissolving celluloid in acetone. Most formulations contain additional ingredients to promote strength and fast drying. I generally don't care to use these because of their odor and weak bonding, but you may find them ideal. Use these adhesives on wood; they are not very satisfactory for metal or styrene plastic, but will work on the few older acetate-plastic kits still available. Satisfactory results can be obtained by applying the cement to one of the parts to be joined, adding the other part, and letting the assembly dry. Better joints can sometimes be obtained on porous surfaces, if a thin coat is applied to both parts, allowed to dry, then another thin coat applied to one part just before assembly.

Plastic cements

These are available in several consistencies ranging from that of syrup to water. The latter, sold in glass jars with an applicator brush, are specifically for styrene and not suitable for other uses.

The biggest problem with styrene cement results from using too much, since the softened plastic will ooze out of the joint and spoil adjoining surfaces. Apply a thin coat to each surface to be joined, let dry slightly, then join the parts.

Save all scraps of plastic and put them into a small container filled with acetone. For safety's sake, be sure the container has a tightly fitting cover. The acetone doesn't dissolve the plastic completely, but after about 48 hours, it has softened the plastic to a putty-like consistency that makes an excellent filler. It will dry in a minute or so, depending on how thickly it's applied. With a small knife, it can be formed to any shape while still soft. This putty is quite useful for filling unsightly gaps and joint lines on plastic models.

Use EDC (ethylene dichloride) for joining Lucite, Plexiglas, or other acrylic plastics. This is a watery liquid and is easily applied to a joint while the parts are held together. Capillary action makes the liquid flow into the seam. This cement does not seem to etch acrylics, so you don't have to be very careful when ap-

CAPILLARY ACTION WILL SPREAD A DROP DOWN THE SEAM.

plying. Plastruct has a blend of this liquid called Weld-On which is used for bonding ABS plastics.

White glue

White resin-emulsion adhesive is sold under trade-names "Elmer's Glue," "Magic Cement," and others, and is known generically as white glue. It comes in a polyethylene squeeze bottle with a pin-hole spout, making it very easy to handle. White glue dries almost transparent, hence it is most useful for adding clear parts such as lamp lenses to a finished model. It will not etch plastic or damage painted surfaces, and is water-soluble until dry. Excess cement can be wiped off with a damp cloth if you work rapidly.

It's best to follow directions and apply a thin coat to each surface, clamping until dry, but a bond can be achieved with a single coat and pressureless drying. It will dry more slowly than most other glues, but the joint will be very strong. Use white glue for joining wood and for installing cloth sails.

Aliphatic resin

This adhesive is similar in uses and applications to white glue. It is yellowish in color, and packaged almost identically. This adhesive catalyzes and sets up faster than white glue. The clean-up is the same.

Contact cement

Goodyear's "Pliobond" and Walther's "Goo" are typical resin-type contact cements. They can be used for joining metal parts, and are applied to both surfaces to be joined, allowed to dry until tacky, and then the parts assembled. These adhesives are messy to use and their very nature requires that their use be limited to the assembly of flat surfaces. Final hardening may take months. They are useful for cloth or leather, but white glue's rinseability makes the latter more satisfactory.

Rubber cement

This is used both in tire repairs and for various office tasks and is similar to contact cement. Its main usefulness to the ship modeler is in making temporary bonds, as in attaching patterns to wood or metal. After the parts have been cut out, the patterns can be peeled off and any remaining cement rubbed off with your fingertips.

Epoxy

Epoxy is greatly overrated as an adhesive for general use. Epoxy cures rather than drying like a glue and is better suited for bonding

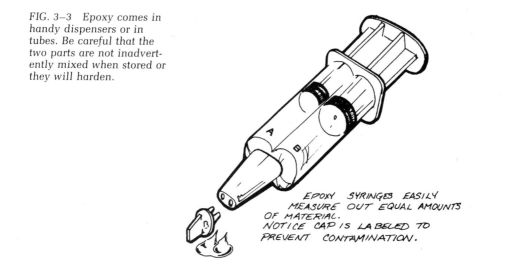

FIG. 3–3 Epoxy comes in handy dispensers or in tubes. Be careful that the two parts are not inadvertently mixed when stored or they will harden.

EPOXY SYRINGES EASILY MEASURE OUT EQUAL AMOUNTS OF MATERIAL. NOTICE CAP IS LABELED TO PREVENT CONTAMINATION.

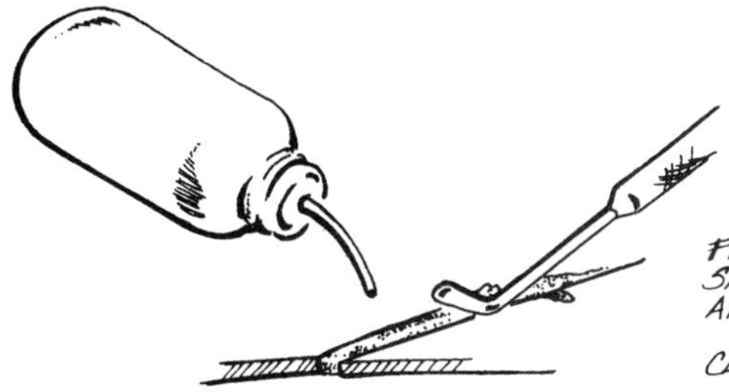

FILL CRACK WITH BAKING SODA
SMOOTH WITH TOOL
APPLY ACC SPARINGLY

CAUTION: FUMES ARE TOXIC!

non-porous materials such as metal or glass. It is generally marketed in matching tubes which are mixed together in a one-to-one ratio. Be careful that you don't leave any on your skin or get it in your eyes.

FIG. 3–4 *An exceptionally strong bond can be created and large gaps can be filled using ACC (Hot Stuff, Krazy Glue, etc.) and baking soda. Do not inhale fumes and be sure to work in a well-ventilated area.*

Hot Stuff/Crazy Glue

These are a fairly new type of adhesive which set up in the absence of air rather than by exposure to air as with glue. They were originally designed for use in surgery to close cuts without stitches, and are designed to bond flesh on contact; be careful or you will be caught up in your work! If you should glue your fingers together, soak them in acetone until they can be gently pried apart. Don't try to pull your fingers apart or you'll rip the skin.

You can mix Hot Stuff with baking soda to form a hard fillet or to increase the effectiveness of a butt bond. If you use respect when dealing with these adhesives, they'll become an important part of your modeling.

KITBUILDING

4

Most model shipbuilders are introduced to the hobby by building plastic kits although a few have the nerve, and money, to dive into a wood model. Perhaps this chapter should be considered as kitbashing, because I feel that every kit requires some detailing to make it more realistic. However, you can build a very credible model using the techniques outlined in this book.

Take the time to learn the basics of model-building and become proficient with them before undertaking a more serious project. Properly building a kit requires considerable skill and, too often, the modeler forgets the most basic rule—read the instructions first!

The best type of kit for the beginner is one of the simplified kits offered by Revell or Monogram. These usually have excellent instructions and easy (relatively speaking) assembly with pre-formed rat lines. The instruction sheets will also help you become acquainted with the names for most of the components of a ship.

Getting started

Read the instructions before you start working. Ships are extremely complicated and even the experts require guidance. You could build yourself into a corner if you are not careful. For instance, many kits require that the deck be glued to the inner side of one-half of the hull prior to hull assembly, while others require the hull to be assembled first. After awhile, you may become proficient enough to skip around, but be patient for now. I will frequently see ways to short-cut kit steps, or to create sub-assemblies for painting, but I still use that printed sheet as reference. Who is more knowledgeable about a kit, after all, than the manufacturer?

The assembly instruction sheet can be used to determine if you have all of the necessary parts and as a checklist during construction. Open the kit immediately after purchase and check for missing or seriously damaged parts. Nothing is more frustrating than to be missing a critical part when a project is coming to an end late at night on a weekend.

Incomplete kits

If the kit is new, most dealers will replace it without any hassle. If you've had the kit for awhile, and it is partially assembled, then you may be out of luck. Most manufacturers are pretty good about replacing missing parts or even parts you may have damaged during construction. Send the part number, kit number and some type of proof of purchase with a SASE large enough for the parts. It won't hurt to include a dollar or two for handling plus a pleading note.

If the kit is rare, don't panic; it's relatively simple to fabricate or repair most parts using techniques from this book. You may also find a similar part from another, less rare kit or from the scrap bin you should be keeping.

Construction

Gather all the tools you feel you might need and set them up in a clean, well-lit work area away from the main stream of other

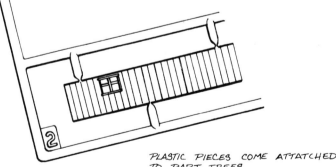

FIG. 4–1   All plastic parts are molded to trees.

PLASTIC PIECES COME ATTATCHED TO PART TREES.

FIG. 4–2 Cut or snip parts off the molding sprue rather than twisting them off. Twisting causes the parts to tear or distort.

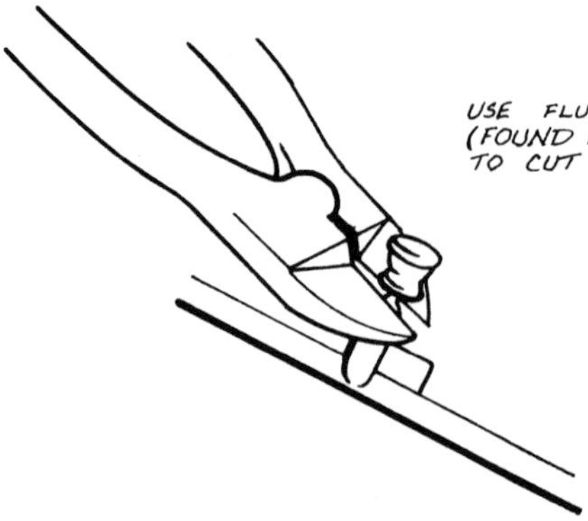

USE FLUSH-EDGED CLIPPERS (FOUND AT ELECTRICAL SHOPS) TO CUT PARTS FROM TREES.

activities. Spread all the parts out and take inventory as mentioned before. Check the parts and decide now if you want to modify or replace any of them with more detailed items. Many hobby shops have ship detail pieces which are available individually.

Cut the parts free from their trees only as you need them, to help you identify them and keep smaller parts from getting lost. You may also find that it's easier and faster to clean flash off of small parts and paint them while still attached to the tree. The tree is better than any device for holding very tiny, repetitive items such as tackle blocks and belaying pins.

Filing

All parts should be test-fit prior to assembly. Hold each pair of pieces up to a light and check for a uniform line of light. File or sand the parts until little or no light is visible and they fit together tightly. This procedure will ensure a good glue joint and will result in less finish-work prior to final painting.

A file has many teeth which remove material by scraping or abrading the surface. Lift the file on each back stroke and press lightly on the forward stroke. Never use heavy pressure or you'll clog the file teeth. Don't use any pressure on the back stroke or you'll dull the filing edge.

Keep the file teeth clear at all times to get the smoothest surface with the least amount of effort. A tool called a file card (not the cardboard type) with wire bristles can be used to keep the file like new. Run the bristles into the file grooves along their length until all foreign material is gone.

Before filing seam lines or putty, allow the area to dry thoroughly. Otherwise, you'll clog the file and get a rough, uneven surface which will have to be sanded smooth later.

Scribing

Most ship kits can benefit from scribing to simulate panel detail or planking. Manufacturers can save a considerable amount of money by simulating planking and paneling with raised rather than depressed lines. They cut the detail into the female dies at the last minute after the shape has been established. If they were to try and cut away everything but the fine, raised lines required to produce a depressed line in the model, it would take many more hours of work.

Most new modelers scribe using the sharp side of the blade

FIG. 4–3 Planking can be scribed with a knife or saw.

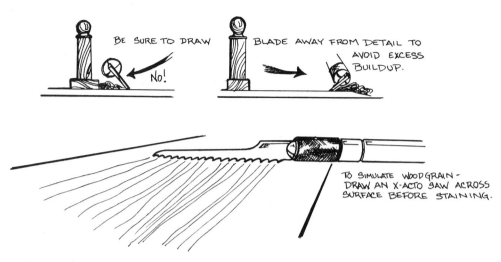

FIG. 4—4 The proper technique for drawing the blade across the surface.

FIG. 4—5 Scribing should be done with the back side of a broken blade. Note that the sharp edge (bottom left in the illustration) displaces plastic and leaves ridges.

and feel that this technique will produce a sharp line. Actually, the reverse is true. The sharp tip tracks like a needle in a record groove and creates a V-shaped valley with edges higher than the surrounding plastic. Usually, they have to sand the scribed area smooth and retrace their lines several times before good results are obtained.

To make a good scribe, break the tip off of a knife with a pair

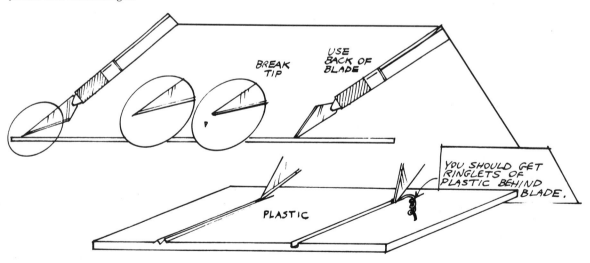

FIG. 4–6 *Here's a special tool you can make for scribing planking rather than using a knife.*

A GOOD ETCHING TOOL CAN BE MADE BY SNAPPING THE HEAD OFF A NEEDLE AND MOUNTING THE BODY INTO A DOWEL.

of pliers. Use the back side of the tip, keeping the knife nearly vertical, and drag it gently across the surface, using a straightedge for guidance. If you're using the right amount of gentle pressure, you will have a continuous curl of plastic ahead of the blade. The line thus produced will be rectangular in cross-section without any raising of the surrounding surface. The finished model will look a lot cleaner and crisper. Experiment on a scrap piece of plastic to get used to the procedure and to see how much better it will look.

Saw cuts

Start cut lines by lightly dragging the saw blade backwards over the edge of the part to create a slight nick. Press on the forward stroke to engage the cutting teeth and take firm, even strokes. After the initial cut, lift the blade slightly on the back stroke to keep from dulling the teeth.

FIG. 4–7 *The quickest method for cutting plastic is to scribe it and then snap along the score line.*

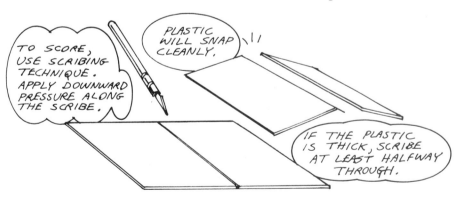

TO SCORE, USE SCRIBING TECHNIQUE. APPLY DOWNWARD PRESSURE ALONG THE SCRIBE.

PLASTIC WILL SNAP CLEANLY.

IF THE PLASTIC IS THICK, SCRIBE AT LEAST HALFWAY THROUGH.

Sheets of plastic can be cut up quickly by scoring. Scribe lines into the plastic using many shallow cuts over the same line until you've cut one-third of the way through. Never use force to speed up the work; one slip with a knife as sharp as an X-Acto can cut you severly. Place the scribe line over a sharp table edge and apply pressure to snap the plastic along the line. Most types of plastic will break cleanly, but acrylic and Plexiglas may shatter. If the edge is too rough, clean it up with #320 sandpaper mounted on a smooth surface such as glass.

Assembly

Hold two parts together and apply a drop of liquid cement or Hot Stuff at the top corner (assuming this is a plastic kit). Capillary action will draw the glue into the seam, making a good solid joint. Don't use too much glue, or you'll weaken the joint and soften the plastic. Hold the parts together for a few seconds or clamp if necessary. Allow 24 hours for the glue to dry thoroughly, or the solvent will leech out and ruin your good paint job.

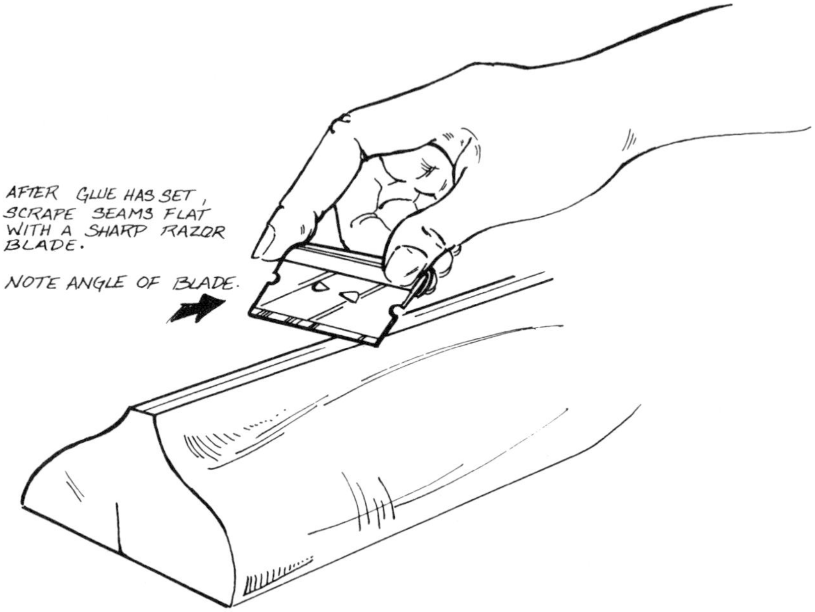

FIG. 4–8 Glue can seep out of joints and leave sloppy seams. Use a knife, razor blade or scraper to clean the edge.

AFTER GLUE HAS SET, SCRAPE SEAMS FLAT WITH A SHARP RAZOR BLADE.

NOTE ANGLE OF BLADE.

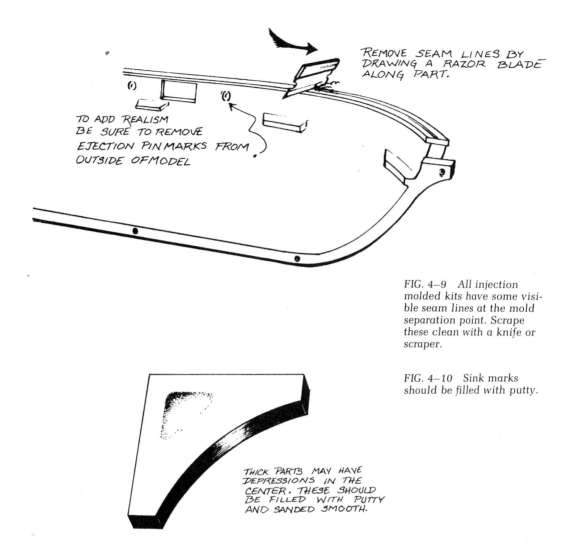

REMOVE SEAM LINES BY DRAWING A RAZOR BLADE ALONG PART.

TO ADD REALISM BE SURE TO REMOVE EJECTION PIN MARKS FROM OUTSIDE OF MODEL

THICK PARTS MAY HAVE DEPRESSIONS IN THE CENTER. THESE SHOULD BE FILLED WITH PUTTY AND SANDED SMOOTH.

FIG. 4–9 All injection molded kits have some visible seam lines at the mold separation point. Scrape these clean with a knife or scraper.

FIG. 4–10 Sink marks should be filled with putty.

Finishing

All models will have ridges or seam lines which can be filed, sanded smooth or scraped with the back edge of a knife blade. Depressions or dimples can be filled with spot putty and sanded smooth. Various kinds of putty are available depending on the size of the hole to be filled. Refer to the sections on painting, detailing, and putties for more details on finishing your model to museum quality.

KITBASHING

5

Kitbashing can produce unique models and is the closest you can get to scratchbuilding with plastic models. I enjoy this type of modeling because it gets fast results, produces a unique model and requires quite a bit of imagination, skill and a little blind luck.

Kitbashing (cross-kitting) can be used for virtually any phase of modeling. You are essentially working with shapes and it doesn't matter if that shape is a plastic salt shaker or a curler pin as long as it represents what you want. I enjoy telling people what some of the weird items are on my models.

If you are planning a conversion of any type, it's wise to stick with kits of the same scale or at least close to one another. It's possible to get away with some variance in scale proportions part of the time. The conversion of the Revell tug uses parts from model trains (1/86 scale) and model tanks (1/72 scale) even though it's 1/96 scale. I feel the visual proportions are close enough.

The tugboat conversion is typical of what can be done. The reason I chose this project is that the Revell tug is always available in one guise or another, so this example will always be current. The results of the conversion can be startling.

Planning

You must start your model by carefully planning out each step. Decide what you're going to use as a base kit and try to determine how to best approach the conversion. I decided that the hull from

FIG. 5–1 The Revell tug boat is used as the basis for the trawler conversion.

the Revell kit was perfect for my fishing boat, but there were many problems as well.

Obtain all the research material possible before buying the first kit or part. Try to determine what parts are the most important to the overall appearance of the finished model. In our case, that would be the hull, cabin house, and masts. These primary items determine the silhouette, or profile, of the model. The other detail items are important too, but these are usually available or can be readily made from scratch. The idea here is that you are creating a jigsaw picture without all of the parts.

Buy the kits you will need to build the completed model. Generally, you wouldn't want to use more than two kits. Being a professional, I usually buy as many kits as I feel will get the job done quickly, because the kits are cheaper than paying labor costs. You will have to decide whether or not the expense offsets the

FIG. 5–2 *The fishing trawler bears little resemblance to its tug boat origins.*

ease of building the model. A collection of catalogs will probably help you make a decision on which models to scavenge.

Lay out all the kit parts and decide which ones to use as is and which to modify. Isolate the parts which will definitely be used and place all of the other parts in a scrap bin. You will be amazed how handy a parts bin will be on future projects of this type. I've been collecting parts for so long that I have a huge cabinet with drawers designated as to type, shape and scale of the parts. I would be lost without these parts.

Try to use the kit instruction sheet as much as possible when building the primary shape. The less modification you have to do, the better. Basically, you will be building the model in much the same way as a stock kit. The tug conversion we show here is considered to be radical because of the vast changes, and yet it is barely more difficult than a stock model.

Once the model is under way, you should follow the appropriate sections of this book for any changes. For instance, you may want to vacuum-form sails for a model that doesn't have them or duplicate cannons for a Man-O-War. As your skills improve, you will probably find this type of modeling very enjoyable as an alternative to scratchbuilding.

Fishing trawler

The fishing trawler is probably the most common type of ship in the world, and yet it is not often modeled when compared to the big square-riggers. The obvious answer for the question "why not?" is that the big ships are glamorous, while the fishing ships are pedestrian and commonplace. Frankly I prefer the smaller vessel because I can include more interesting detail. I feel that the day-to-day ships have more character than the sailing ships or battleships. Besides, I prefer to build something different from what others are doing.

The hull is basically stock, but the kit's deck planking is both out of scale and poorly detailed. Assemble the stock hull halves without the planking. Trace the outline of the deck onto a piece of typing paper and glue it to scribed sheet styrene from Evergreen Plastics. Cut out the deck and glue it in place of the original. Fill in all the molding sink marks using body putty.

Many of the deck details came directly from the tug, but you

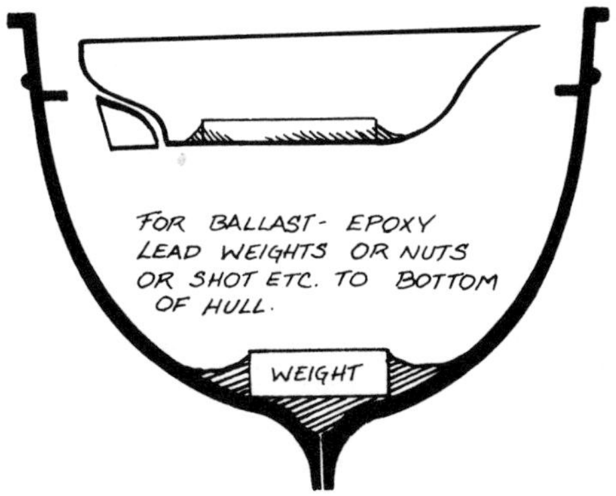

FOR BALLAST- EPOXY LEAD WEIGHTS OR NUTS OR SHOT ETC. TO BOTTOM OF HULL.

WEIGHT

FIG. 5–3 Ship models tend to be top heavy. Add weights to the bottom, inside the hull to ensure that they will sit right.

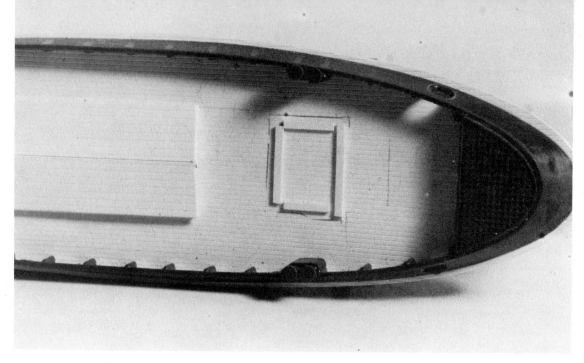

FIG. 5–4   Evergreen scribed styrene can be used to replace the stock decking.

FIG. 5–5   Canvas can be simulated by using surgical tape.

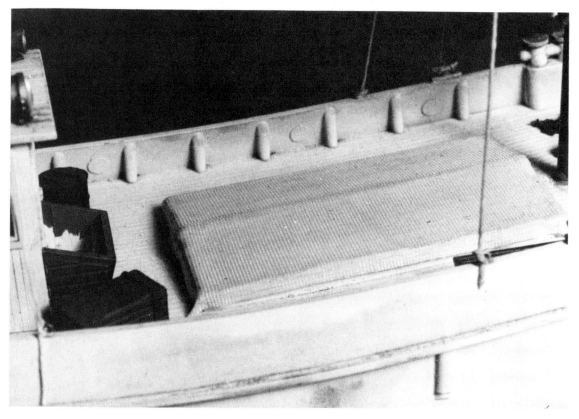

FIG. 5–6   The deck house was made from a variety of train parts.

FIG. 5–7   If the cabin top is made removeable, it will ease building and allow for display later.

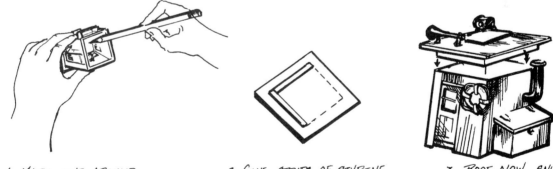

1. MARK LINE AROUND
   INSIDE OF CABIN ON
   UNDERSIDE OF ROOF

2. GLUE STRIPS OF STYRENE
   ALONG LINE

3. ROOF NOW SNUGLY
   FITS ONTO CABIN

FIG. 5–8 Fishing net can be simulated with hair net, heavy stockings, or wedding veil material, stained with acrylics.

FIG. 5–9 The light lens is reflective, but a grain-of-wheat bulb could be used to light it.

FIG. 5–10 *The seagull is actually a pigeon.*

may want to use parts from another kit. Build the hatch out of strip and sheet styrene. The canvas was made using surgical tape (Dermicel), although you can also use facial tissue applied with a liquid cement appropriate to the materials you're using, i.e., white glue for a wooden model. The stack, windows, nuts and bolts are all model train parts in styrene from Grandt Line Products. These items, as well as hundreds of others, are available from any good model train shop or mail order from Walthers. The anchor, rope, steering wheel, and belaying pins all came from a hobby shop specializing in model ship parts.

FIG. 5–11 *The trawler is the same scale as the trains, and they will be combined in a diorama.*

The cabin house was built using the same scribed sheet styrene as the deck. The construction is a little tricky because of the curved, slanted deck it has to fit. I cheated a bit by using a small strip of styrene as an edge molding to hide the seam, but I still had ensure an approximate fit. The way I did this was to cut a template out of paper. It's far easier to keep trimming a template to fit than it is to trim away at a piece of plastic. A small machinist's square is valuable in keeping the walls of the cabin perpendicular with the waterline. It can also be used in truing up the masts later.

I wanted the roof of the cabin house to be removable, so that I could put in a fully detailed interior later. The roof was fitted so that it looked right on the outside. I then marked a line around the inside with pencil to locate the walls. Small, short strips of styrene were glued just outside of the line so that they put pressure against the wall, giving the roof a force fit; it can be taken off and put back on at will. You will appreciate this feature when it comes time to paint the model.

The detail bits come from all over. The coffee-can-shaped light is a brass item from Cal-Scale trains. The masts are wood turnings, but you could also use kit masts from another model. The rudder is part of an HO-scale Walthers weather vane. The life preservers, row boat and oars are from Campbells train parts in HO. The sea gulls are actually pigeons from Walthers.

Eventually, this model became part of a model train layout complete with Campbell's wharf and small dockside switcher trains. When the time comes, I will have to cut the hull off just below the waterline so that it can be set in an ocean of artist's acrylic gel.

SCRATCHBUILDING

6

The techniques described here are well within anyone's capabilities. However, these are usually not utilized by the average modeler and should not be attempted until you are thoroughly familiar with modeling basics.

Whenever you have modified a kit to any great extent, you are really into scratch work. At what point does one become the other? It's very difficult to determine. Technically, a scratchbuilt model can be considered to be one which doesn't use any commercially available parts in its construction. However, anyone would be foolish to machine cannon barrels out of solid brass when there are so many available.

Wood carving

Wood carving is sometimes necessary as a step toward achieving another end. I'll frequently carve a shape out of a hardwood such as bass or gelutung and use it as a master (buck) to produce a vacuum-formed piece, a fiberglass shell, or as a base to add planking.

A good set of woodworking tools from a craft shop are essential. You will need several sizes and shapes of chisels, a plane, a hobby knife, files, a Surform, and possibly a Dremel moto-tool.

Rubber molds

The method to make rubber molds for relatively small parts is easy. The best type of mold material in general use is Silastic "A."

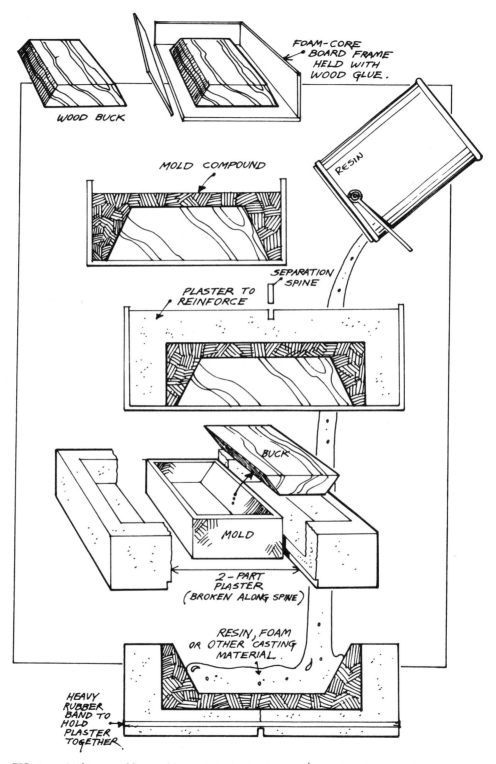

FOAM-CORE
BOARD FRAME
HELD WITH
WOOD GLUE.

WOOD BUCK

RESIN

MOLD COMPOUND

PLASTER TO
REINFORCE

SEPARATION
SPINE

BUCK

MOLD

2-PART
PLASTER
(BROKEN ALONG SPINE)

RESIN, FOAM
OR OTHER CASTING
MATERIAL.

HEAVY
RUBBER
BAND TO
HOLD
PLASTER
TOGETHER.

FIG. 6–1   Making a rubber mold is relatively simple if this procedure is followed.

Whether or not you are using a kit-based or a scratchbuilt master, you must first block off all holes that go through the piece. Use water-base clay, not an oil-base clay to fill the undercuts, since it will not retard set-up time on the rubber.

The next step is to build up a box around the part using illustration board or poster board, which can be acquired at any stationery or art supply store. White glue such as Wilhold or Elmer's works perfectly with the board. The box should leave one inch around the top.

Fill the box with table salt to the desired depth of about ½ inch over the top of the part. Pour the salt into a paper cup and mark the level with a pencil line. Now you will know exactly how much mold material to use. Be sure to clean out all excess salt from the mold and cup.

Mix the rubber according to the directions and slowly pour it into the box (Fig. 6–2). Gently shake and/or tap the box to bring

FIG. 6–2 Pouring the rubber compound into the box.

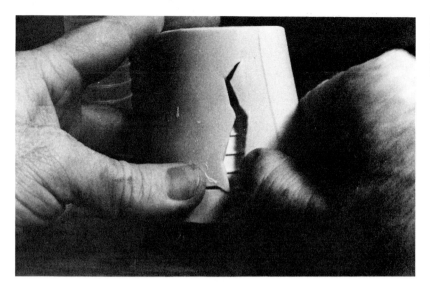

any air bubbles to the surface. Let it set for about 24 hours or as recommended by the manufacturer.

When the rubber has set up completely and is firm, remove all the illustration board. Don't worry about trying to save the board, it's not worth it.

For actual casting use casting resin which has been warmed up to about 80 degrees F. For very complicated parts, it is sometimes best to paint the resin into the mold halves before putting them together and pouring in the remainder. For best results, let the resin set up completely (over night) before opening the mold.

Lost wax casting

The first step in this method requires the preparation of a wax master, or pattern, from which the mold will be made. Using wax and a warm spatula, the part is shaped exactly the way the finished part will look. Pins and small pieces of wire and scrap can be used to shape the pattern. Use dental wax, which can be purchased at dental supply houses. This wax comes in sheets about ¼ inch thick.

Work as much detail as you need into the pattern since this process can be used to get the finest of details. If you plan to use the finished mold more than once, make sure to angle (draft) the parts so that they will pull out of the mold easily. If the part is

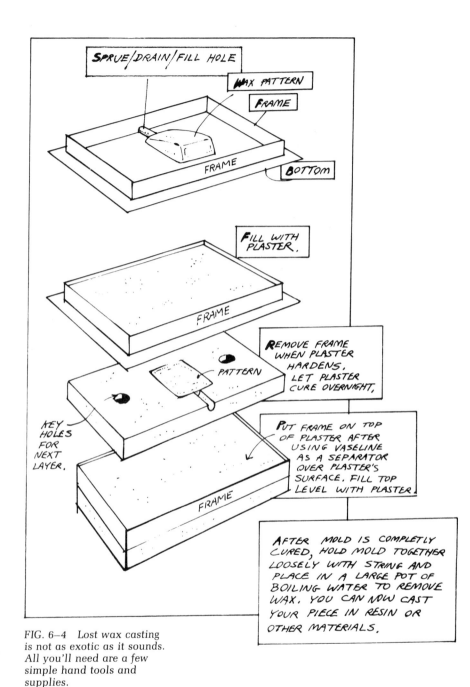

SPRUE/DRAIN/FILL HOLE

WAX PATTERN

FRAME

FRAME

BOTTOM

FILL WITH PLASTER.

FRAME

PATTERN

REMOVE FRAME WHEN PLASTER HARDENS. LET PLASTER CURE OVERNIGHT.

KEY HOLES FOR NEXT LAYER.

FRAME

PUT FRAME ON TOP OF PLASTER AFTER USING VASELINE AS A SEPARATOR OVER PLASTER'S SURFACE. FILL TOP LEVEL WITH PLASTER.

AFTER MOLD IS COMPLETLY CURED, HOLD MOLD TOGETHER LOOSELY WITH STRING AND PLACE IN A LARGE POT OF BOILING WATER TO REMOVE WAX. YOU CAN NOW CAST YOUR PIECE IN RESIN OR OTHER MATERIALS.

FIG. 6–4 Lost wax casting is not as exotic as it sounds. All you'll need are a few simple hand tools and supplies.

complex, you probably will be just as happy to break up the mold to get the part out.

Place the finished pattern on the sheet and form a box around it to form one half of the mold. Place the part face down and pour in a mixture of plaster of paris. The plaster should be sifted to get out lumps and should be mixed with enough water to pour easily. When buying this plaster, get a package of plaster hardener to make a stronger mold.

Allow the mold half to cure and dry at least over night. It can then be removed from the box and the base can be taken off. The wax pattern is embedded in the plaster and is turned so this side is up.

Gouge two holes on either side of the wax pattern. These gouges will be filled with plaster when the second half is poured and will act to line up the mold halves.

Place the mold frame on top of this first half to make the second. Dust the mold surface with dry plaster to help part the halves when finished. Pour a mixture of plaster into the frame and again allow to cure.

At this point, you have the finished mold with the wax pattern inside. Tie the halves loosely with string and put the whole works into a pot of boiling water. The wax then becomes "lost" as it melts out of the mold cavity. All the sharp and fine details are left in a clean and undisturbed cavity.

Make the part by taking powdered dental plastic and mix it with thinner. Both can be obtained at dental supply houses along with hints and tips on their use. Make a thick putty and poke it into the cavity, making sure you have enough to fill. Close the mold and press it together. Heat the mold at 150° in an oven to cure the plastic. Allow the part to cool and carefully remove it. Use the part as you would any plastic piece.

Resin casting

Casting resin is a transparent liquid plastic that upon curing gives glass-like, clear castings. Casting resin can be a useful material for the hobbyist, as well as for professional use. Success is achieved by those who work slowly and carefully and keep the molds and equipment clean. With experience you'll acquire ability and gain speed. Practice first with simple molds, then try more detailed forms. Use flexible molds that will bend or stretch to release the casting or use plaster and metal molds, the latter as either a one-piece mold that will release the casting, or a two-piece mold.

The surface of your mold will be reproduced in reverse in the casting, i.e., an indented scratch in the mold will produce a raised line in the casting. A dull surface mold will produce a dull surfaced casting; a highly finished surface will produce a like surface with less need for polishing.

Equipment
A glass jar or any similar container will do as a mixing jar. A medicine dropper and a tablespoon are suitable for measuring. Any clean rod or stick may be used as a stirring rod. These can be cleaned later with acetone.

Molds
Plaster molds, flexible rubber molds, and metal molds can be made using techniques described elsewhere in this book.

Mixing
Measure the resin with a tablespoon. To each two tablespoonfuls of resin (two tablespoon = 1 ounce) add five to ten drops of hardener. Stir the two together thoroughly, then allow to stand for a few minutes. Break remaining surface bubbles with a pin.

Preliminary setting
Use a clean, dry mold coated thinly with a film of soap, furniture wax, or mold release. Some mold releases can be brushed on the surface of the mold to prevent sticking or bubbles. Pour the resin in slowly to allow any bubbles to rise to the surface.

When resin cures, there is a chemical interaction which creates its own heat. If the right proportion of catalyst has been added, this chemial heating will occur within 15 to 30 minutes. It is one of the critical times in the procedure, for if the chemical interaction is too great, the casting will get too hot and cracks will appear in the casting. If the casting has not started to set-up after two hours, then the casting should be slightly warmed to start the action. This problem would indicate that too little catalyst was used.

It is usually better, if time is not of great importance, to allow your casting to set over night or for two to three days to slow cure.

Final curing
When the casting has jelled and is apparently solid, it should be heat cured. This will fully harden the casting and eliminate any

stickiness. An oven temperature of approximately 200 to 250 degrees F. will be ample. The length of time needed could vary from thirty minutes to two hours, depending on the size of the casting. Check the piece periodically.

Removing cast part

Release the top edge of the casting with a knife and tap the mold gently on the bottom until the casting falls out. With flexible molds simply flex the mold and remove the casting.

If the casting still has a sticky surface, it can be hardened with additional heating. This sometimes happens because the surface exposed to the air is neutralized and does not get proper chemical action.

After it has completely cured, resin can be sawed, sanded, and polished like any plastic. Holes can be drilled with ordinary metal drills. Resin will take a high polish; even castings from glass molds will take an added gloss when buffed by hand or machine.

Fiberglass

Fiberglass is loosely matted or woven textile material which is bonded with a liquid plastic resin. The fabric is saturated with resin which has been catalyzed. The resin then sets up hard. Resin by itself is quite brittle, but with the fiberglass reinforcement it becomes very strong.

Materials

LAMINATING RESIN. Polyester materials are quick, easy, and economical to use; they form a protective coating and strong bond. They may be used on most any clean, dry surface except redwood, cedar or Styrofoam.

Used as an undercoat in all kinds of fiberglassing, it is primarily designed to act as a binder for the fiberglass fabric. Like all polyester resin, the laminating type requires a catalyst; however, even when cured, it remains tacky and is not "dry" to the touch. Additional coats of resin may be easily applied to the cured laminating resin without having to sand or rough the surface.

FINISH RESIN. Used as a final, protective, waterproof coating over the laminating resin, finish resin usually contains a small amount of dissolved wax which floats to the surface and thereby causes the resin to dry tack-free. Finish resin can be easily sanded. Should you wish to apply multiple coats of finish resin, you must sand between coats.

FIBERGLASS PUTTY.   This is a polyester resin material which requires a catalyst. It is used for filling cracks, dents, deep scratches, or for repairing holes. White or green in color, it can be painted or covered with fiberglass.

EPOXY RESIN.   Epoxy resin is more expensive than polyester but will provide an exceptionally strong, permanent bond and protective coating. Epoxy may be used on almost any clean, dry surface including redwood, cedar and Styrofoam.

Epoxy resin is used both as an adhesive base coat under fiberglass cloth and as a protective finish coat. It dries to a high gloss, tack-free surface. Additional coats may be applied without sanding.

FIBERGLASS CLOTH.   Fiberglass cloth is a heavy, woven fabric resembling drapery material. The weave is fairly loose and very orderly. It is generally white in color and is sold in various weights and weaves. Model-building is done with the lighter weight materials which are thin.

FIBERGLASS MAT.   This is a non-woven material consisting of chopped strands which are laid out in a blanket in a random manner. The fibers are held together by a light binder. Mat is also white and is supplied in various weights. The 2-ounce weight is the most common.

FIBERGLASS TAPE.   This is a woven reinforcing fabric tape sold in 2-, 4- and 6-inch widths. The tape is used for a positive seal at joints and seams on large items, but may be used on its own for a model.

Preparation

Preparing the surface to be coated is important to ensure a good bond with the fiberglass. Remove oils with a non-oily solvent such as alcohol, or dishwashing detergent. Fill small cracks with fiberglass putty. Be sure surface is perfectly dry.

Polyester laminating

1. Cut a piece of fiberglass cloth the size of the area you wish to cover.

2. Using a measure of two ounces per square foot of area, pour the amount of laminating resin needed into a disposable container. (Do not use a plastic or wax-coated container for this purpose.) Never mix too much at a time as pot life at 70 degrees is only about 30 minutes. The mixture cannot be used after it starts to gel.
3. For each ounce of resin add one drop of catalyst (hardener). If temperature is above 70 degrees use less catalyst, if below 70 use more catalyst.
4. Mix thoroughly until consistent.
5. Divide surface into workable sections. Pour catalyzed resin on to one section at a time and spread with an old paintbrush. If first coat soaks in, apply a second coat.
6. Starting from one end of surface to be covered, lay the fiberglass cloth into the wet resin and smooth out with your fingertips. Work out all trapped air by pushing the bubbles out from the center toward the sides.
7. A second coat may be necessary to fill weave of cloth. Start at one end and apply catalyzed resin over the cloth, saturating thoroughly and working air bubbles out to edges.
8. When resin is firm, but before it becomes completely hard, trim edges to desired size with a sharp knife or razor blade.
9. Allow to cure completely for at least eight hours. Sand fiberglassed surface to remove all imperfections before applying finish resin.
10. If color is desired, add colorant to finish resin and stir thoroughly. Following manufacturer's instructions, color all the resin you intend to use.
11. Pour finish resin into a disposable container and add one drop of catalyst per ounce of resin. Mix well.
12. For best results, flow on finish resin with a minimum of brushing. Two or more coats may be required to obtain a smooth surface. It is not necessary to let the resin cure between coats. If allowed to cure, sand lightly before applying next coat.

Epoxy resin

The surface preparation, laminating and finishing steps are the same with epoxy resin as they are for polyester materials. The only difference in using epoxy is in the mixing. This is important, as proper cure depends on following the directions carefully.

1. Measure accurately, with equal parts of resin to curing agent.
2. Mix together thoroughly and stir vigorously for at least two minutes.
3. Immediately pour entire mixed contents onto surface. If material is left in the container, it will set up very quickly. Once it is mixed, the working time is approximately 30 minutes. For best results, epoxy resin should be used at room temperature.
4. Additional coats may be applied without sanding between coats.

Cleanup
Clean all tools and brushes with cleaner or acetone. This should be done as soon as you are through to prevent resin from hardening on them.

Metal die-casting

Most people prefer the look, heft and durability of metal parts over plastic. You can create your own metal parts after first making a master from any material.

The first step is to create a rubber mold as described earlier in this book. You'll need a two-part mold to form one solid three-dimensional piece. This isn't as difficult as it may sound. Support the object to be molded on straight pins to keep it off of the box base, or surround it with water clay. Fill the box to the halfway point on the object and let it cure for six to eight hours.

Spray the object and the rubber with mold release, to form the break line for the mold. Pour in the remainder of the rubber to cover the object and let it cure again six to eight hours.

Strip the box away and separate the two halves. Look for any imperfections. Cut vents to allow air and gas to escape from the mold. Don't worry about the metal coming out of these holes; even if it does, they can be filed off later.

A large cutout will be the pour hole for the molten metal. This should be quite large and positioned in an area where it can easily be filed away later.

The metal I use is nothing more than 60–40 coreless solder. It comes as bar stock from any hardware store and a few dollars' worth is enough for several figures.

You need a disposable pan to heat the solder to its melting

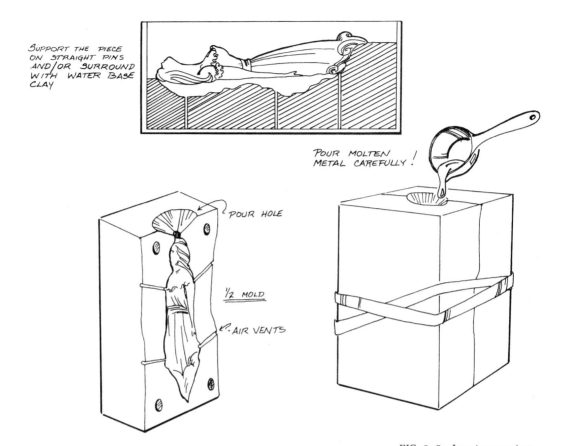

SUPPORT THE PIECE ON STRAIGHT PINS AND/OR SURROUND WITH WATER BASE CLAY

POUR MOLTEN METAL CAREFULLY!

POUR HOLE

½ MOLD

AIR VENTS

FIG. 6–5 Low temperature metals allow for home casting white metal figures and parts as good as commercial items.

point. Caution: *Do not use the pan for food after using lead solder.* Be extremely careful of the molten metal or severe burns could result. It may take a few minutes for the metal to melt, so put it on the stove before proceeding with the next step. Don't worry about using too much, as the excess can be re-melted later for another object.

Wrap the mold with rubber bands to hold it together. Use a vise as well if the object is large. The mold could expand, causing distortion.

Stand the mold upright and slowly pour in the molten metal. Use care so as not to burn yourself. If the object being formed is large or the rubber thick, heat the mold in an oven set at 200 degrees prior to filling with lead.

Wait several minutes for the object to cool slightly. If you are too eager, there could still be molten lead in the mold or the object will warp. If you want more than one object, pour it now while the mold is still hot. It will save you a lot of trouble later and the image will be sharper. *Do not inhale toxic fumes* from the rubber.

Finish the object as you would any commercially cast item, and you'll have a truly unique item.

Modeling with heat

Every modeler learns a set of tricks to speed up the construction of a plastic model or to improve on the finished product. Sooner or later the one area that acts as a stumbling block to even the most experienced builder is that of extensive modification and reshaping.

There are several products on the market intended for use as a body putty, but these all have serious drawbacks. The first is a long curing time between each layer. You can hasten this time by heating the plastic under a lamp or in an oven, but you may run the very real risk of warping the surrounding plastic. Quick curing can cause the putties to shrink and crack as well. If too much putty is used, then the area that has been re-worked will sink after the model has long been finished.

Another problem is the putty's density. All the putties on the market now are porous and require special priming and sealing before a good finish coat can be applied. I have had models ruined because the re-worked area appeared dull and flat compared to untouched areas.

The obvious solution is to use a material as close to the original styrene consistency as possible. One solution has been to dissolve chips of styrene in acetone to use as a putty. The problem here is that the solution takes a minimum of three days to cure, and the acetone base crazes the surrounding plastic.

The use of heat to mold the plastic appears to be the only quick and easy solution. Melting the plastic will make it pliable and easy to shape. Two pieces of styrene can be welded together into one piece that is many times stronger than a glue joint. The beauty of this is that the joint or body work will be ready for a finish coat or sanding in 30 seconds!

Obviously care must be taken when using this method. Too much heat will melt all of the plastic beyond repair or at least warp it, causing a lot of unnecessary work. The fumes from melting plastic are toxic and can make you nauseous, but it beats the toxicity of glue.

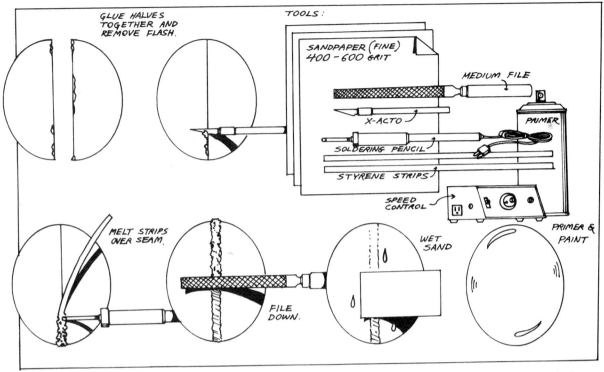

TOOLS:

SANDPAPER (FINE) 400 - 600 GRIT

MEDIUM FILE

X-ACTO

PRIMER

SOLDERING PENCIL

STYRENE STRIPS

SPEED CONTROL

PRIMER & PAINT

MELT STRIPS OVER SEAM.

FILE DOWN.

WET SAND

FIG. 6–6 *Pieces of plastic can be heat-seamed together with a hot knife or soldering pencil.*

Plastic putty

There is no easier way of filling minor seams, molding lines or imperfections on a model than with the use of putty.

Auto body filler putty, Duratite Surfacing Putty, Green Stuff, and Duco Lacquer Spot-In Glaze are all excellent for putty work on models. Duratite surfacing putty is available in hobby shops and hardware stores. Green Stuff and Duco Spot-In Glaze are obtainable from automotive parts houses and paint stores handling automotive paint supplies.

A small artist's spatula can be used for applying putty to the model. These are available from art supply stores. The spatula method is the best, as it gives the smoothest application and reduces the chances of the formation of air bubbles.

When applying putty, be sure to apply in thin layers and build up an excess, as it shrinks while drying. If you are using putty for contouring, spread it far enough back on the body to allow the contour area to flow smoothly.

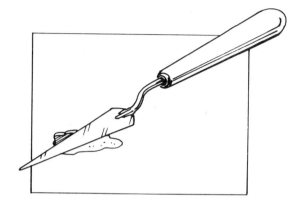

FIG. 6-7 Putty can be applied easily with an artist's spatula.

Putty should dry for at least eight hours for the best bond. Shape area to general contour with a file. When the general shape is achieved, sand the area with #400 wet-and-dry sandpaper to semi-smoothness. Remember to sand carefully, as putty is cut away faster than plastic by sandpaper. X-Acto's contoured sanding blocks are a great aid. When the area has been worked smooth by sanding, apply a couple of coats of primer. This will show up air bubbles, holes, pits, or any other imperfections. Re-apply putty to fill imperfections and set aside to dry for eight hours.

Wet-sand the area again; apply another couple coats of primer to check finish. You may find that still another application of putty is needed. Time and patience are the most important items in the building of a professional looking model. When the area is free of imperfections, wet-sand to final finish. Prime entire model and prepare it for paint.

Soldering

Soldering can be used for the assembly of brass parts or to hook-up lighting wiring. The proper technique is very simple to learn and should be included in your repertoire of skills.

The equipment required for soldering is simple and relatively inexpensive. Soldering pencils (irons) can be purchased for less than nine dollars. An expensive gun, such as the dual-range Weller, is not necessary to do a satisfactory job. In fact, some people find it to be too bulky for this type of work. X-Acto sells a combination soldering pencil and hot knife which works great. Other soldering irons (gun- or pencil-type) are made by Ungar, American Electric Heater Co., and Hexacon Electric. In choosing an iron, be sure the tip will allow you to heat the work piece rapidly with a minimum of heat loss at the tip. For extensive work on large objects, a heavier tip is better, since the amount of heat stored at the tip is greater.

Both unplated and plated tips will produce good results if they are properly maintained. Unplated copper tips should be removed from the iron frequently for cleaning. To remove oxidation build-up (scale), the tip should be filed while cool. The file should be a flat, fine, single-cut tooth-type, such as a jeweler's Swedish file (X-Acto).

Tin the tip before using by applying solder to the working surface as soon as it reaches soldering temperature. Plated tips should be maintained by wiping the tip on a wet sponge and retinning as previously described. Discard the tip when it can no longer be tinned. Clean either tip by wiping on a wet sponge after each soldering operation, to prevent a build-up of flux.

FIG. 6–8   A good solder joint should be sturdy but not loaded with excessive solder.

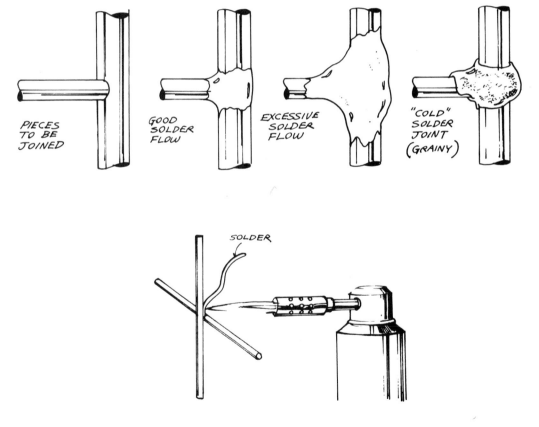

Flux is a honey-like liquid used to help clean the metals being soldered and promote the flow of solder. Flux fumes are toxic and should not be inhaled. Be sure your work area is well-ventilated. The flux should be a non-corrosive type, such as Sal-Met's.

The most commonly used solders are tin alloy, lead-tin alloy, lead alloy, and silver alloy. The most popular type is a lead-tin alloy of 60 percent tin and 40 percent lead. Ersin's Multicore solder contains five cores of non-corrosive flux, which makes it one of the most useful solders on the market. When aided by Sal-Met flux, it makes soldering a virtual snap.

Thoroughly clean the pieces to be joined with steel wool and denatured alcohol. Spread a minimal amount of flux on the surfaces to be joined. Apply heat at the intersection of the joint until the flux begins to bubble. Rosin-core flux becomes active and removes oxides only when the metal has reached soldering temperature. Since the flow of solder is determined by solder size, select one which will provide easy control for the amount required. I've found that size 18 S.W.G.-.048 inch works best for me.

Feed small amounts of solder to the joint until a good fillet is achieved. Do not apply more solder than is required to fill the joint. Too much solder results in a weak joint. Avoid melting solder against the iron and flowing it onto a surface which hasn't been sufficiently heated. When enough solder has flowed, remove the solder wire, leaving the iron in place. Keep the iron on the joint for a couple of seconds to boil out any flux or impurities.

Remove the iron with a wiping motion, taking care not to disturb the joint. Allow the solder to cool completely before con-

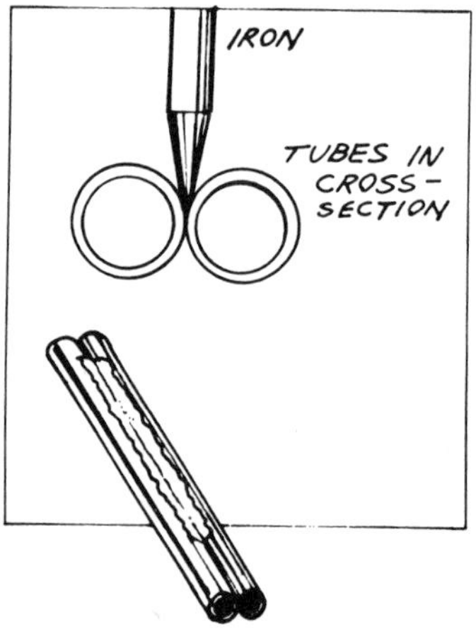

FIG. 6–9 *Adjacent pieces can be soldered together even if they do not have flat edges to be matched.*

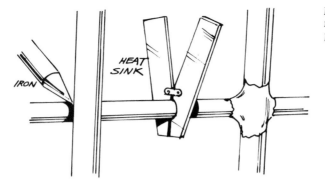

FIG. 6–10 *A heat sink will radiate heat away from a previously soldered joint.*

tinuing. A typical good solder joint will be bright and smooth, with solder feathering out to a thin edge from the main body of solder. The joint will also be free of pin holes, craters, cracks, fractures, spikes, excessive solder bulges and flux pockets. If the joint is disturbed while cooling, it will appear dull gray and rough textured.

When soldering intricate parts, it becomes necessary to isolate the original soldered connections to keep from weakening them due to the additional heat. A heat sink is designed to radiate heat from unwanted areas and to keep the area cool enough to prevent solder from flowing into unwanted areas or from softening. Place heat sinks between any existing joints and the working area, and solder in the normal manner. An alligator clip can be used as a heat sink in an emergency.

Flux residue should be cleaned from the parts within four hours after soldering, since it will become more difficult to remove the longer it remains. Remove all residue by brushing the parts with a medium-stiff brush (an old toothbrush or the like) dipped in denatured alcohol.

Heat will oxidize brass and turn it a dullish brown color. If you wish to restore the original luster of the brass, simply rub with fine-grade steel wool and alcohol to remove the oxides, and buff with rubbing compound and a soft rag.

Silver solder

Silver solder forms the strongest bond short of brazing and is a better conductor of electricity than normal solder. Most soldering irons won't produce enough heat to melt silver solder. One of the LP butane or propane canned torches such as Westline or Bronson is inexpensive and will last through many jobs before needing re-fueling. A great deal of care should be exercised when using one of these torches. Read the instructions on the can and follow them precisely. Always use them in a well-ventilated area; store in a cool place and *never* puncture or incinerate the can.

Close the valve tightly by turning counterclockwise. Screw the valve, finger tight, onto the fuel tank. Point the nozzle away from yourself or any combustibles, and turn the valve clockwise until a faint hissing can be heard. Hold a lighted match to the end of the nozzle and adjust the valve until a small flame continues to burn. Allow the torch to burn on this low flame for at least a minute to warm up. Don't tip the can until after this initial warm-up. Afterwards, the can may be tilted to any angle with safety. Regulate the valve until you get a flame two to three inches long.

Clean the pieces to be joined with alcohol and steel wool. Apply silver solder flux to both pieces and clamp together. Hold the tip of the flame at the intersection of the pieces.

Apply the silver solder wire to the joint as soon as the flux begins to bubble and flow. Use only enough solder to form a small fillet. You can easily flow solder over a long distance by drawing the flame just ahead of the solder. Allow the soldered piece to air cool before handling. Use heat sinks to isolate joints other than the one you're working on. There are types of low-temperature silver solder on the market that can be used like regular solder, but you sacrifice strength for convenience.

Solder removal

Wicking is the term used for removing excess solder from a joint. A braided or woven strand of wire is covered with flux and placed against the joint. Apply heat to the joint until the solder flows freely. Most of the solder will flow into the braided wire, leaving the area relatively clean. Clean the wicked area with alcohol and a stiff brush. If complete removal of all traces of solder is desired, simply rub with fine steel wool.

Desoldering

Desoldering a joint for resoldering or removal is very simple. Heat-sink the area surrounding the joint. Apply heat to the joint and tug slightly on the wire (tube, etc.) until it pulls free. If you wish to solder something else to the same area, use more flux.

Low-temperature solder

Cerro Metal, sold in hobby shops, is an easily used composition for low-temperature soldering.

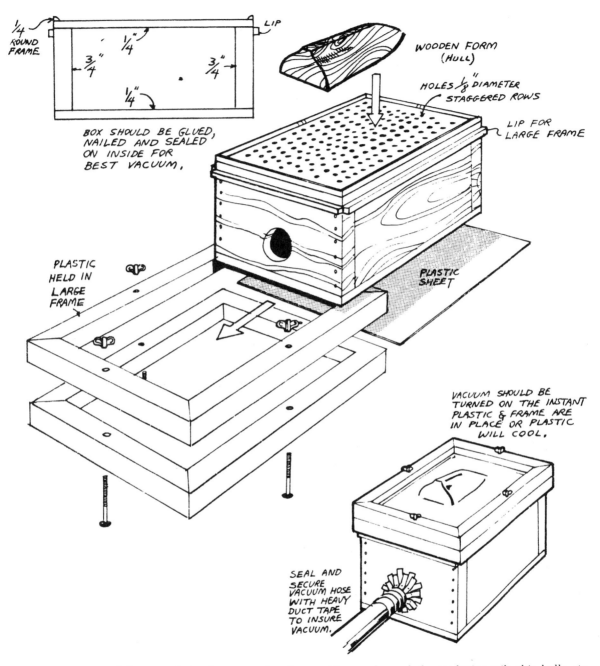

¼ ROUND FRAME

LIP

1"⁄4

3"⁄4

3"⁄4

1"⁄4

BOX SHOULD BE GLUED, NAILED AND SEALED ON INSIDE FOR BEST VACUUM.

WOODEN FORM (HULL)

HOLES ⅛" DIAMETER STAGGERED ROWS

LIP FOR LARGE FRAME

PLASTIC HELD IN LARGE FRAME

PLASTIC SHEET

VACUUM SHOULD BE TURNED ON THE INSTANT PLASTIC & FRAME ARE IN PLACE OR PLASTIC WILL COOL.

SEAL AND SECURE VACUUM HOSE WITH HEAVY DUCT TAPE TO INSURE VACUUM.

FIG. 6–11   A simple vacuum-forming machine can be made for producing sails, thin hulls, etc.

Vacuum forming

Vacuum forming can be used by the average ship modeler to make sails or even hollow hulls. Vacuum forming plastic may sound like a complicated technique, but it's actually quite simple if you have the equipment to do it properly.

You should construct a box as shown in Figure 6–11. A vacuum cleaner provides the drawing power for the forming process. After the box is made, make a master (buck) for the item you want to duplicate in plastic. The object must be no more than a couple of inches tall and can't have any undercuts (areas less than vertical). As many surfaces as possible should have an angle of 5 degrees off vertical to facilitate pulling the mold out without dam-

FIG. 6–12 Sails can be vacuum formed from thin plastic.

age. Make a base ¼ inch high to fit around the molded part to give you excess for a cut line later.

Any of a number of different objects can be used to heat the plastic. The best would be heated coils such as those found in an electric oven. You could use a light bulb, heat gun, hair dryer, area heater, etc. Just be careful that the plastic doesn't start smoking or catch fire. Fumes can be poisonous if the styrene actually burns. Heat the plastic and watch it constantly. Plastic will first wrinkle and draw up, then it will start to drape. It's during the "draping" stage that you want to place it quickly over the form and start the vacuum. If the part doesn't come out with crisp detail, check the amount of draw (vacuum), and try heating the plastic a little longer.

HULL CONSTRUCTION

7

A ship model requires a good solid foundation just as a building does, and that is the basic hull. If you're using a wood kit, the hull is probably rough-shaped already, so you can continue with other sections of this chapter. If the hull is to be built up like a real ship, with the planks directly on a bulkhead or frame, move on to the planking section. However, you may find the techniques described here interesting even though you may not need them until the next model. For the sake of instruction, we'll assume that you are scratchbuilding a model and are starting with a solid block of wood.

Nomenclature

A ship's hull is nothing more or less than functional sculpture with subtle, graceful, artistic and classical lines. Modelers through the centuries have been fascinated with recreating the form and trying to capture the essence of the sailing ship. Shipwrights have also found models useful as engineering tools. Half-hull models were used to help ship-builders in the yard by giving them a visual aid. When it is used as an aid, much of the language of models is unique to engineering. If you are following old plans, it is helpful to know this language. The problem is sometimes further complicated by the fact that one word may have many different meanings. A good case in point is the word "tack." It has no less than five totally different uses! It can be the forward corner of a fore

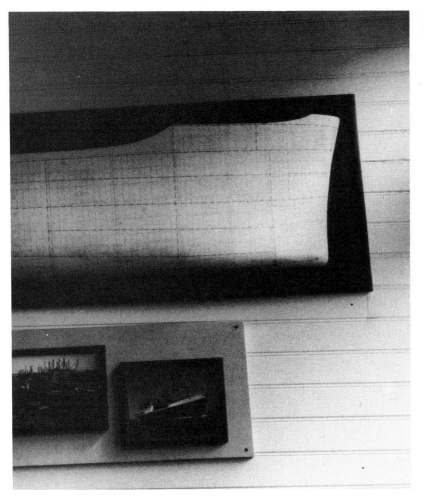

FIG. 7-1 *Half-hull models are used by real shipbuilders as a three-dimensional blueprint.*

and aft sail, a rigging line, a cloth used just prior to painting or varnishing to remove sanding dust, the windward side of the ship, or the course of a ship sailing into the wind.

As if multiple usage weren't bad enough, the spelling is also a problem. Most sailors had a spoken language which was not written down. Their meandering travels put them in contact with many nationalities and dialects. Often as not, words were misinterpreted because of difficulty with pronounciation. The word "trunnel" or "trennel" was actually a contraction of "tree nail," describing a piece of wood dowel used to pin planks to frames.

FIG. 7–2 Note the trunnels, rings, caulking, and planks on this real ship.

The words used throughout this book will come naturally to you as work progresses, but it wouldn't hurt to learn some of the basics now. If you want to follow this book, you'll be forced to learn many words because I'll be using them to avoid any confusion. Refer to the Glossary to help you understand the various words.

Solid hull construction

Many modelers prefer to build the hull from a solid piece of wood, rather than create the shape from pieces. The type of carving wood I prefer is a special hardwood known as gelutung. It has very fine grain, like ash or oak, but is soft and as easy to carve as basswood. However, if the model is to be planked, you can use a cheaper, readily available wood such as clear pine. It is important that the wood you select is free of knots, dry rot or cracks. Otherwise, you'll have extreme difficulty in carving and shaping the hull.

Carefully plan the phases of construction, so that you won't box yourself into a corner later. Take a little time now and try to visualize the work in progress. It might also be wise to establish some goals as to when certain phases will be completed. Mark out the rough shape of the finished hull on the block of wood. Trace the plan views on the top, sides and ends. Make the initial marks slightly oversize to allow for final shaping. Allow for planking by making your marks inboard from the edge by the thickness of the planks.

Shaping the hull isn't as difficult as you might imagine, if you know a few tricks. The most important of these is to establish firm, indelible datum (reference) lines from which all measurements can be made in the future. Don't be like most beginners and make the marks on the outer surface of the wood where they'll be cut or sanded away. If the hull is simple in shape, you can get away with quartering the wood. Cut the block lengthways and sideways forming four rectangular cubes. Make sure too that the hull runs in the same direction as the natural grain of the wood. Mark each of the wood pieces initially, so that they can be reassembled in their original positions.

Sand the mating cut surfaces to make sure they are smooth

FIG. 7–3 Using template to form model from wood.

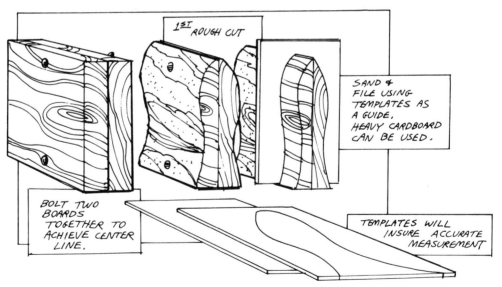

1ST ROUGH CUT

SAND & FILE USING TEMPLATES AS A GUIDE. HEAVY CARDBOARD CAN BE USED.

BOLT TWO BOARDS TOGETHER TO ACHIEVE CENTER LINE.

TEMPLATES WILL INSURE ACCURATE MEASUREMENT

HULL CONSTRUCTION

FIG. 7–4 The cross-sections of a ship can be broken down into the three types shown.

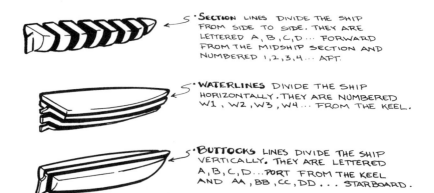

• **SECTION** LINES DIVIDE THE SHIP FROM SIDE TO SIDE. THEY ARE LETTERED A, B, C, D ... FORWARD FROM THE MIDSHIP SECTION AND NUMBERED 1, 2, 3, 4 ... AFT.

• **WATERLINES** DIVIDE THE SHIP HORIZONTALLY. THEY ARE NUMBERED W1, W2, W3, W4 ... FROM THE KEEL.

• **BUTTOCKS** LINES DIVIDE THE SHIP VERTICALLY. THEY ARE LETTERED A, B, C, D ... PORT FROM THE KEEL AND AA, BB, CC, DD ... STARBOARD.

and straight. Test fit each piece and check that there are no major gaps. Dye each of the mating surfaces with dark shoe dye or add a drop of dye to aliphatic resin wood glue. Glue the wood pieces back together and clamp securely until the glue has set for at least 24 hours. It may seem a little silly to cut up a piece of wood and immediately reassemble it, but what you have done is to establish the center lines of the model in such a way that they are permanent. Now you can whittle away at the model and never have to worry about losing the centers.

This procedure can be taken further by slicing up the hull

FIG. 7–5 Solid hulls are shown here being carved using waterline or buttock line profiles. You will need to cut templates for all three planes for the final shape.

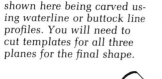

1. CUT BOARDS TO WATERLINE OR BUTTOCK LINE PROFILES

2. GLUE BETWEEN LAYERS. CLAMP UNTIL DRY.

3. CARVE AND DETAIL. SEAMS CAN BE USED AS GUIDES.

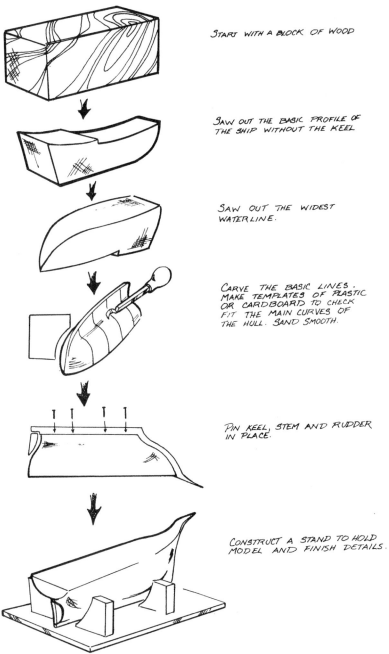

START WITH A BLOCK OF WOOD

SAW OUT THE BASIC PROFILE OF THE SHIP WITHOUT THE KEEL

SAW OUT THE WIDEST WATERLINE.

CARVE THE BASIC LINES. MAKE TEMPLATES OF PLASTIC OR CARDBOARD TO CHECK FIT THE MAIN CURVES OF THE HULL. SAND SMOOTH.

PIN KEEL, STEM AND RUDDER IN PLACE.

CONSTRUCT A STAND TO HOLD MODEL AND FINISH DETAILS.

FIG. 7–6 This is the hard way to form a hull, but it does provide a seamless shell if that's what you're after.

like bologna to correspond to cross-sectional views of the hull shape. Consider the lines to be like those in a topographical map. Each line represents a different level. The individual slices can be shaped to match the drawings before gluing them back together. Then you have to create smooth transitions between the sections. This is the process many nautical engineers use in creating their models. In fact, the individual pieces of wood are alternately light and dark to simplify identification of the levels. A model left in this state can be as attractive as any other type.

If you own, or have access to, a band saw, you can save a lot of time by rough cutting the hull with it. Trace the side and end views on the wood block. Make all cuts at this point at approximately 90 degrees. If you are really daring, and can afford another piece of wood if you make a mistake, then hand-shape the hull on the band saw. Templates can be made out of cardboard or plastic to use as a guide to check progress. Hold the wood tightly and try to rest one edge on the table. Be careful that your hands are not in line with the blade; the wood could catch and draw your fingers into the teeth before you can react. Take small cuts, each time stopping to check your progress against the plans.

Now is the time to mount the hull. One approach is to screw a large block onto the deck. This can then be clamped into a vise or a Work-Mate, leaving the entire bottom of the hull accessible.

FIG. 7-7 Some kits come with the hull already roughed out and require only minor work to finish.

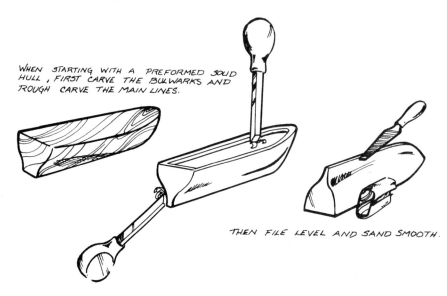

WHEN STARTING WITH A PREFORMED SOLID HULL, FIRST CARVE THE BULWARKS AND ROUGH CARVE THE MAIN LINES.

THEN FILE LEVEL AND SAND SMOOTH.

A spectacular British Man'O War, built from a Revell kit by Ed Lawton. He used a Mini Shop-Mate to hold his model during construction. A swivel-base vise, such as the D-vise, will work well too.

The Yamato, *a Japanese battleship, is from the collection of Fred Hill.*

This Norske Love *was the first model built by Rick Tobias! The fine details in the fittings and armaments are almost breathtaking.*

Modelers often admire the look of a natural wood ship and opt to leave it in its raw state, with just varnish for a finish. Ken Pleis did that with his Golden-brand riverboat, the Delta Queen.

Note the myriad deck furniture in this picture. The rigging and placement of nets may look random and cluttered, but everything has a definite place.

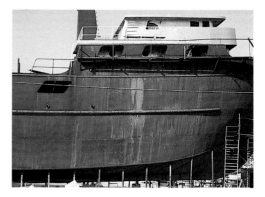

Ship modelers are often reluctant to weather their handiwork, preferring to keep ships in pristine condition. However, when placing models in a diorama, study such boats as this one to duplicate realistic rust and weather effects.

A model boat can be displayed by setting it up on timbers, just like this one in drydock. Note how rusty the steel hull has become from the salt air without a protective coat of paint.

The base for a ship model should be as finely crafted as the model. The base and HMS Bounty were built by Ed Moore.

Believe it or not, this is a Revolutionary War submarine—nicknamed "Turtle" for obvious reasons. Mark McGunegill scratchbuilt this beautiful wood and brass specimen because there were no kit models of this exotic historic vessel.

This interesting and colorful scene could easily be duplicated in HO scale. A Revell tug can be modified into a fishing trawler; the New England-style buildings can be modified from European kits by Faller or Kibris. This real scene is similar to a model layout being built for the author's book, Narrow Gauge Railroading (Chilton Book Co., in press).

Modern fishing boats are very similar to the old-fashioned ones, except for details. This boat has both the new-style plastic net floats and the older cork floats.

Many older ships were literally works of art. Handpainted detail by Ed Lawton on this British Man'O War is time-consuming but rewarding.

Most real commercial boats are painted white because high visibility is desirable; white paint also has the surprising advantages of being less expensive and easier to keep clean!

Small and simple, yet loaded with detail. The Swift, an Artasania Latina-brand kit, is a good starting point for the beginner. It was a fun project for the builder, Owen Bird.

Ripples are evident in even the calmest of waters; when simulating water for a diorama, be sure to include rippling or waves on the surface for realism.

Note the superbly crafted fittings—right down to realistic coils of rope—lying in the bow of this whaling boat by Don Richter.

A fishing trawler, almost "scratchbuilt" by the author, who used a highly modified hull from a Revell tugboat kit, hand made many of the fittings—and bashed a few kits for other realistic details.

Naval ships are almost always painted "battleship grey" with white lettering. The Navy prides itself on keeping its ships clean and shipshape, so don't overdo the weathering. It might be interesting to duplicate recent battle damage: a large-scale 1/32 PT boat is a good choice for detailing of this type.

The screw holes can be filled later, covered with planking or used as mounting holes for the mast. The hull could be placed directly in a vise, but certain areas won't be accessible at all times. As final sanding and shaping progresses, it will be handy to use a swivel-headed vise, such as the Panavise, to be able to rotate the work.

The final hull shape can be further roughed out using a variety of hand tools. A small woodworker's spoke shave can be used to shave off slivers of wood. If you want to be more traditional, use a two-handed draw knife. Be very careful with any tool, as a slip can be very dangerous. Set the shavers so that thin slivers are cut off with each stroke. You wouldn't want to gouge the wood and ruin all of your hard work.

A small plane or Surform is next in line for rough shaping. Use each with smooth strokes and take your time. Check your progress with simple sculptor's calipers. Power tools can be used too; although you have to be careful of the progress. A hand piece, such as the Foredom, with a sanding drum can be used in tight recessed areas. A disc sander powered by a drill or air is great for shaping the broad, sweeping curves. Use 80-grit paper in the beginning and graduate to 220 as the final shape is reached. Reserve final shaping for hand tools only.

Sanding blocks can be made out of a variety of materials or you can use commercially made items. Hard blocks of pine, hard rubber or aluminum are best for broad, flat areas. Soft, pliable materials are good for final sanding, but can cause high and low spots if not handled carefully. Use #320 paper of the non-loading

FIG. 7–8 A simple jig to hoid the model will make work easier.

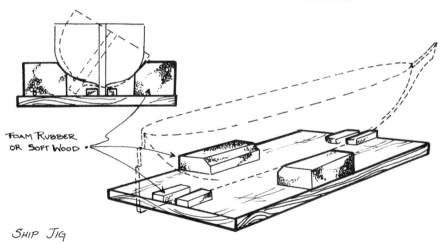

FOAM RUBBER OR SOFT WOOD

SHIP JIG

type, which is usually white in color. The tan papers are cheaper, but load up too quickly and cause uneven sanding. The black, more expensive, wet-and-dry papers are good but they also load up too quickly. Never wet-sand a wood model as you would plastic or metal. The wood will absorb too much water and cause serious problems when the grain is raised. Don't try to substitute other liquids either. I once thought that alcohol could be used on painted wood, but I nearly destroyed a good model in the experiment.

After all work on the bottom of the hull is done, cut blocks of foam rubber or a soft wood such as pine to create a holder for the keel. Screw the blocks in place to hold the model in a vise as before. Create templates for the deck contours and use them as you work. The deck is usually not as complicated as the hull but most will be contoured in two directions to allow for drainage.

FIG. 7–9 *Building a boat is good basic practice for building the ship later because it is easier and uses the same procedures.*

Laminated hull

The laminated hull is simply an extension of the techniques already described except that the hull is built up side to side and

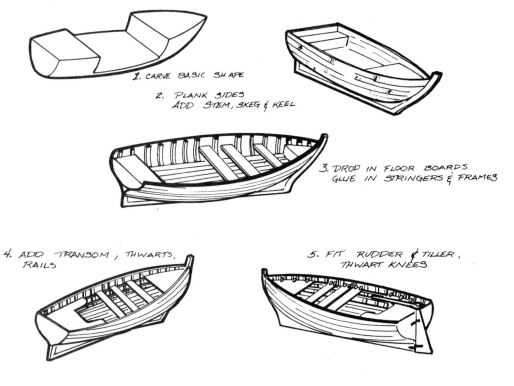

1. CARVE BASIC SHAPE

2. PLANK SIDES
   ADD STEM, SKEG & KEEL

3. DROP IN FLOOR BOARDS
   GLUE IN STRINGERS & FRAMES

4. ADD TRANSOM, THWARTS, RAILS

5. FIT RUDDER & TILLER, THWART KNEES

for and aft like a large jigsaw puzzle. You will have a hollow model when complete. The biggest advantage is that pieces for each side can be cut and shaped at one time, assuring a perfectly symmetrical model. Great care in creating the profile of a ship is important, because this is what is most often viewed in model form and on real ships. It's rare for anyone to look at a ship head-on in such a way that they can detect asymmetrical lines.

After all the stepped pieces are glued together, blend them together into a smooth shape, using the wood tools described earlier in this chapter for a solid hull model. You'll find that shaping the hull this way is fast and simple.

Plank and bulkhead hull construction

In some ways, this method can be simpler than others, since you are going directly to the planking stage after the cross-sectional pieces are cut. It also approximates the real procedure for building a ship. The only method closer to prototypical would be actual plank-on-frame, as used on Admiralty models. These were used as engineering and sales tools, and had to be wholly accurate. I can't imagine anyone wanting to go to the trouble involved with plank on frame construction, since the work will be hidden by planking and decking.

The first step in plank and bulkhead construction is to cut the keel according to plans. Determine how many bulkheads will be used, their spacing and thickness of material. The keel must be sturdy because the rest of the model depends on its strength. It would be a good idea to sand the keel to its final shape now when there isn't anything else in the way. Once the planks are in place, you'll have to work around them.

Cut notches in the keel corresponding to the thickness of the bulkheads. Make the cuts halfway down since they will interface with corresponding cuts in the bulkheads, much like egg-crate construction. I prefer to use a table saw or radial arm saw for these cuts, since I can control the width and depth of the cuts, and I know they'll be square. If you do the cuts by hand, use a sharp mitre saw and mitre box to ensure straight cuts. It's best to make the cuts as tight as possible for a firm fit. I actually measure mine so that they are a few thousandths of an inch shy, but my equipment is accurate enough to allow for this.

It would be a good idea to make a waterline template before

gluing any of the bulkheads in place, otherwise the planks won't fit properly. Glue the bulkheads in place using Aliphatic resin instead of white glue. Check the alignment in all directions before the glue sets up. If possible, try to clamp the pieces in place as they set. Set the model aside to dry for 24 hours before proceeding.

Once the glue has set up, blend the bulkhead edges as you would the solid block on a solid hull model, otherwise the planks will be uneven on the finished model. Check progress often to make sure the planks will be smooth. A wood rasp is a good tool to use for initial shaping.

Planking

Ah, the moment of truth! Planking is very much in evidence on a ship, almost as eye-catching as the masts and rigging. It's important that the planking be straight, accurate and clean. Regardless of hull construction, planking is almost always done using the technique described here. The only alternative would be to scribe the planking in, but that is difficult and obvious.

A ship's planking is made up of many different widths and thicknesses of boards. Cheaper kits never show an accurate representation of this, since it represents a lot of extra effort and expense in tooling. The modeler wishing to build a model in a hurry can use pre-scribed wood, but the effect will not be as realistic as with individual planking.

Real deck planks were laid side by side parallel to the keel along the length of the ship, each course or layer being referred to as a strake. Thicker planks were used in some areas of the deck to act as waterways between the timberheads.

Inboard of the waterways is the nibbling strake. This is planking which is the same thickness as the rest of the deck planking, but it is notched for those planks which were laid square with the keel. The parallel deck planking is cut off square on the ends to fit into the notches in the strake rather than tapering to a sharp point. Many models are shown the latter way, but it is generally inaccurate. Openings in the deck had facing planks fitted, which took up any irregularities in fit and allowed for a better caulking seal.

When planking, start at the main wale and place the remaining planks from there. Tape can be useful in determining the correct shape and layout of each plank. Be aware that equal width planks laid precisely edge to edge will tend to flare out at the stern and

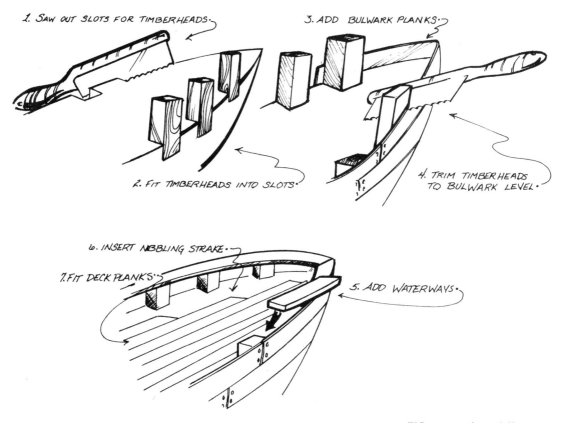

1. SAW OUT SLOTS FOR TIMBERHEADS.

3. ADD BULWARK PLANKS.

2. FIT TIMBERHEADS INTO SLOTS.

4. TRIM TIMBERHEADS TO BULWARK LEVEL.

6. INSERT NIBBLING STRAKE.

7. FIT DECK PLANKS.

5. ADD WATERWAYS.

FIG. 7–10 *If you follow set procedures, building the timberheads and waterways will be relatively simple.*

converge at the bow. You can accomodate this in a number of ways that will be accurate, but it is best to use the approach described in the plans you're using.

It is possible to plank most of the hull with untreated wood, since most of the curves are gradual. However, it will probably be impossible near the bow or stern. You could steam the wood

FIG. 7–11 *A typical waterway is constructed as shown.*

WATERWAY

and bend it over the hull while it dries, but there is an easier way. Soak the wood in ordinary household ammonia until it sinks. At this point, the fibers are fully saturated and can be bent readily. Work in a well-ventilated area, because ammonia is a severe bronchial irritant. Use straight pins or bug pins to hold the planks in place on the hull and let them dry for several hours. When dry, the wood will be permanently set and can be glued in place without any special clamping or fitting.

Bulwarks

Bulwarks are the sides between the upper rail and deck. On most ships, this area is open, exposing the timberheads and upper parts of the frame. On naval gun ships, this area was planked like the outside but with light, narrow wood: the purpose being to offer additional protection against cannon balls. This latter style is a little easier to build since you can use scribed wood and finish off the model without the hassle of fitting each of the exposed timberheads.

Construction of the bulwarks is dependent on the technique used in creating the hull. If the hull is solid, and it is a naval ship, simply add the entire top section. If the hull is solid, but the bulwarks are exposed, cut into the hull and add the timberheads individually. In most cases, kit instructions will show you how to best approach this problem. If you're building from scratch, take time to plan the model carefully, and you will be able to avoid a lot of trouble.

Decking

Decking the ship varies little in technique from planking the hull. The only difference is in the layout of the wood and plank size. You can either use pre-scribed wood cut to the proper shape at the nibbling strakes or use individual strips of wood. I prefer the latter because the grain and color varies slightly from board to board, making the finished model appear more realistic.

Most people prefer to start the decking at the centerline and work out. There is something to be said for this, because it doesn't give you odd-sized nibbling strakes.

Pre-stain each of the deck planks before gluing them to the model. Any glue on the wood seals it, preventing you from staining it later. Also, the boards will appear slightly variegated, enhancing the "individual board" look. Use white glue or aliphatic resin, and lead weights to secure the boards while the glue sets. Allow

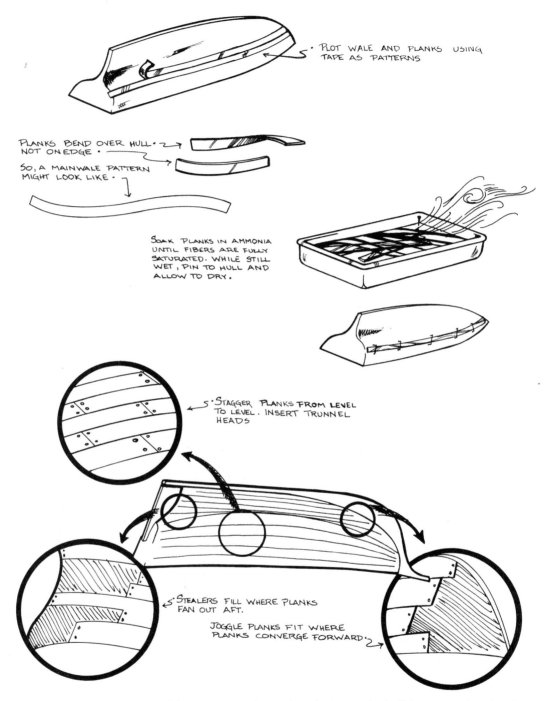

PLOT WALE AND PLANKS USING TAPE AS PATTERNS

PLANKS BEND OVER HULL. NOT ON EDGE.

SO, A MAINWALE PATTERN MIGHT LOOK LIKE.

SOAK PLANKS IN AMMONIA UNTIL FIBERS ARE FULLY SATURATED. WHILE STILL WET, PIN TO HULL AND ALLOW TO DRY.

STAGGER PLANKS FROM LEVEL TO LEVEL. INSERT TRUNNEL HEADS

STEALERS FILL WHERE PLANKS FAN OUT AFT.

JOGGLE PLANKS FIT WHERE PLANKS CONVERGE FORWARD.

FIG. 7–12 Many modelers steam wood to make it form over the hull, but ammonia is far simpler. Be sure to work in a well ventilated area.

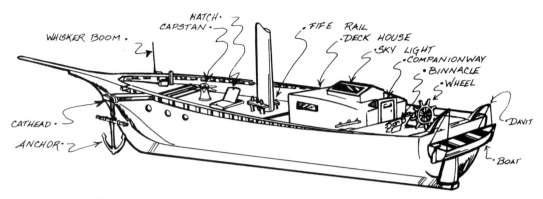
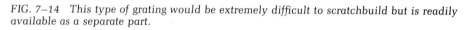

FIG. 7–13 These are typical items of "furniture" which may be found on a modern ship.

FIG. 7–14 This type of grating would be extremely difficult to scratchbuild but is readily available as a separate part.

the glue to set up for at least a half hour before removing the weights.

Finish the ends of the outer planks square, rather than tapering them all the way to the end. This shape and plank are known as the nibbling strake. On real ships, this shape made it easier to fit the planks and allowed for more efficient caulking of all seams (Fig. 7–2).

Waterways are the outermost planks near the edge of the ship. These were made out of thicker wood than the other planks so as to form a waterway. On naval gun ships, they were chamfered to accommodate the wheels. On all other ships, they were normally finished off square.

FIG. 7–15 Canvas can be simulated by using tissue soaked with white glue or with surgical tape.

Holes were cut into the bulwarks to allow water to drain off. On most ships, these had hinged doors that opened when water pressure was exerted from within and closed when pressure came from the sea. These were called scuppers, and many model ship supply companies offer castings at a reasonable price.

There really isn't much to be said about building the bow or stern of a ship that hasn't already been covered in other areas of the ship's construction. It's simply a matter of following the kit instructions or referring to the plans if you're scratchbilding.

Furniture

The equipment on board a ship is referred to as the furniture. It can include everything from a simple hatchcover to a full deckhouse. Virtually all of a ship's furniture is available from model ship suppliers. It would be a waste of your time, money and resources to try and build most of these items from scratch. There are a few items though that might be worth the effort.

A simple hatchcover as used on a merchantman can be made

FIG. 7–16 Skylights are available as commercial items from a number of manufacturers.

out of scribed wood or individual boards. The hinges can be bought at a model train or ship store. Batten down the hatch using heavy thread defurred in beeswax. The various hooks and eyes can be bought at a craft shop.

A hatch battened down with canvas can be easily simulated. Cover the wood with tissue paper held in place with white glue thinned in water. Simulate the eyelets by painting a dot of silver every few scale inches. Thread should be glued at the painted

FIG. 7–17 Model train and doll house hobby shops are excellent sources for detail parts such as railings and wood turnings.

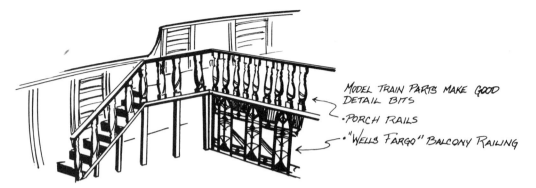

MODEL TRAIN PARTS MAKE GOOD
DETAIL BITS
• PORCH RAILS
• "WELLS FARGO" BALCONY RAILING

FIG. 7–18   Model train parts are used for detail.

FIG. 7–19   Boats can be made solid and covered with planks and canvas.

dots to simulate tie-downs. The simulated canvas can be painted with thinned acrylics.

Skylights can be simulated in a variety of ways. Model train companies such as Walthers, Campbells, and Grandt have built-up skylights available as separate items, or you can use windows and build the frame. Obviously, you can also fabricate the whole thing using strip wood and clear styrene.

Many of the fancy railings and decorative ironwork on a ship

FIG. 7–20 Many modelers prefer boats open to expose the interior construction.

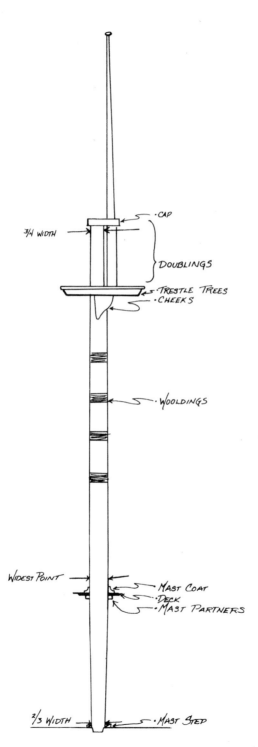

FIG. 7–21 Tall masts were made in two or more parts because they were limited in height by trees from which they were cut.

·CAP

¾ WIDTH

DOUBLINGS

·TRESTLE TREES
·CHEEKS

·WOOLDINGS

WIDEST POINT

·MAST COAT
·DECK
·MAST PARTNERS

⅔ WIDTH

·MAST STEP

can be found in a train shop, if not a model ship shop. The train items are meant to be porch railings, building scrollwork and filigree, but there is a wealth of different styles suitable for ships. There are even acid-etched pieces in brass which are miniature works of art.

If you want to be authentic, you can create artwork in black ink for the actual ironwork and have it custom-etched. I've done this for movie models and the results are outstanding—but a little expensive. Look up shops under the headings Chemical Milling, Acid-Etching or Printed Circuits in your Yellow Pages.

Cannons can be turned on a miniature lathe, but you are better off buying them ready-made unless you're a purist or can't find a suitable match. Operating a lathe and milling machine is beyond the scope of this book.

Boats

It is confusing to a lot of people, but ships carry boats. A rowboat is carried on most sailing ships and is usually hung on davits or lashed to the deck. If you intend to leave a boat lashed in place, or want to cover the open part with canvas, these are simple to make. Carve them out of solid wood and cover the open side with tissue soaked in white glue to simulate canvas. If you want to

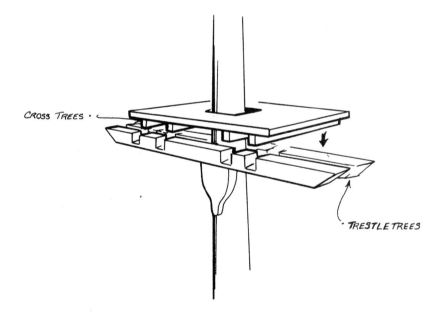

CROSS TREES

TRESTLE TREES

FIG. 7–22 Trestletrees and cross trees were used to lengthen masts.

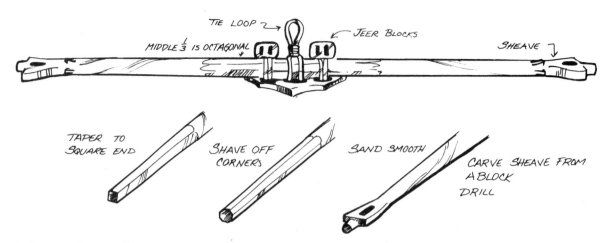

FIG. 7–23 Spars will have
to be carved from dowels as
shown.

show accurate detail, the boat will be as difficult, and will use the
same procedures, as the ship itself. You may be lucky though and
find a suitable match in the ready-made commercial items.

Masts, spars, yards, and gaffs

Masts are often referred to as spars. They were made out of the
straightest tree trunks obtainable and were therefore limited in
height to the highest tree. On ships where more height was essential, spars were doubled and tripled with caps, cheeks, trestle
trees, doublers and cross trees. In other words, the various spars
were lashed together to form longer spars.

Most of the hardware bits are obtainable, but they are also
easily made. The spars themselves can be made out of doweling
or square basswood stock. Carve the stock down until it has the
proper taper and is nearly round. Rough-shape it further with 80-
grit paper and gradually work down to 320-grit paper to finish.
You may want to chuck up the dowel in a drill to speed things
along, or shape it on a wood lathe if one is available.

RIGGING

8

Rigging is without doubt the focal point of most models. It is the first thing that most people notice. To the uninitiated, the various lines, cables and chains look like they are randomly placed. To the knowledgeable person, they all have a logical, necessary function.

Basically, rigging serves to keep the masts upright, the spars suspended and maneuverable, and the sails so they can be furled and unfurled. If you study various photos or plans of real ships, you'll be able to see what every line is meant to do. While you're rigging the model, remember that form follows function and it won't seem half as complicated or mysterious.

Almost any model can benefit by a little extra time and effort spent in rigging. Years ago, most of the plastic kits came with outstanding rigging and instructions. Today that story has sadly changed. People are in too big a hurry to take the time to tackle such a job. The same kits that impressed me as a child now offer simplified hull construction and rigging. One blurb on a box cover even has the nerve to announce that the model can be built over a weekend! To me this detracts from the long-range enjoyment and the shorter term satisfaction of building the model. Why bother?

The procedures described here can be used to vastly improve any model. The fact that new models have been made so simplistic means that there is even more room for improvement than before. It's not difficult to replace the cast plastic ratlines with hand fab-

ricated ones. The kit's rigging is usually simplified, so a little research will show you how to improve the model with more rigging lines. Much of the ship's furniture can be replaced or added to with commercial parts. I once saw a Revell Constitution which had been customized this way, and it looked fantastic! You'll be

FIG. 8–2 Standing rigging
uses heavier rope than running rigging.

amazed at how little effort it takes to place a plastic model in a
category close to that of a scratchbuilt.

Rigging is clearly broken down into two categories. If you
tackle each of these separately, the work will go quickly and easily
and make complete sense.

FIG. 8–3 Shrouds and stays can be made out of finer thread and twisted into shape.

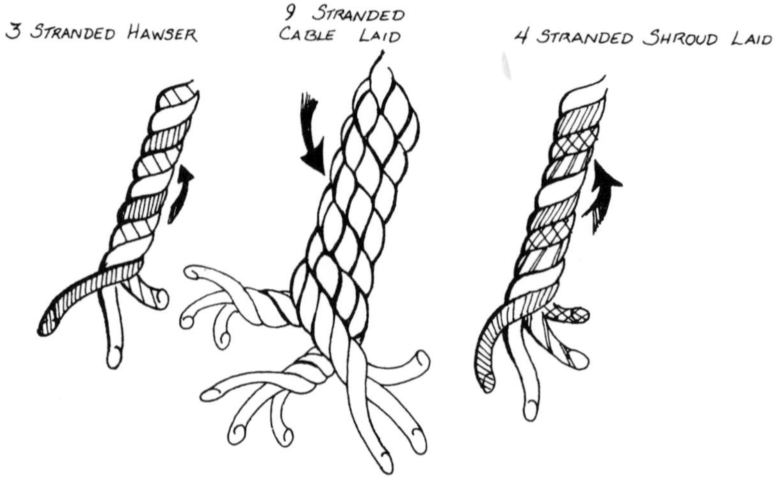

3 STRANDED HAWSER

9 STRANDED CABLE LAID

4 STRANDED SHROUD LAID

Standing rigging

The standing rigging is responsible for keeping the masts and bowsprit upright and in-line. The thread you use should be heavier for this rigging than for anything else. The rope used on real ships is cabled into diameters up to two inches. The shrouds may be slightly larger than the stays on many ships. Shrouds and stays are usually permanently installed and are preserved with tar or creosote—thus being black rather than brown.

FIG. 8–4 Masts are always stabilized by triangulation of the shrouds and stays.

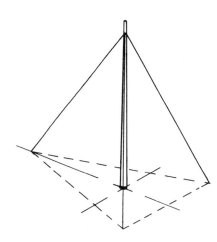

MAST SYSTEMS WERE STABLE BECAUSE THEY WERE BASED ON A PYRAMID.

FIG. 8–5 Deadeyes and lanyards are used to keep lines taut. Note the dark color and heavy rope.

FIG. 8–6 Ratline rigging need not be as complicated as it looks. This is one simple technique that is fairly realistic.

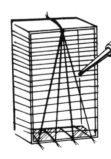

1. WRAP SHROUDS VERTICALLY AROUND FRAME AND TIE OFF. WRAP FOOTROPES HORIZONTALLY.

2. PUT A DROP OF GLUE AT EACH JUNCTION POINT

3. CUT FREE OF FRAME AND TRIM LOOSE ENDS.

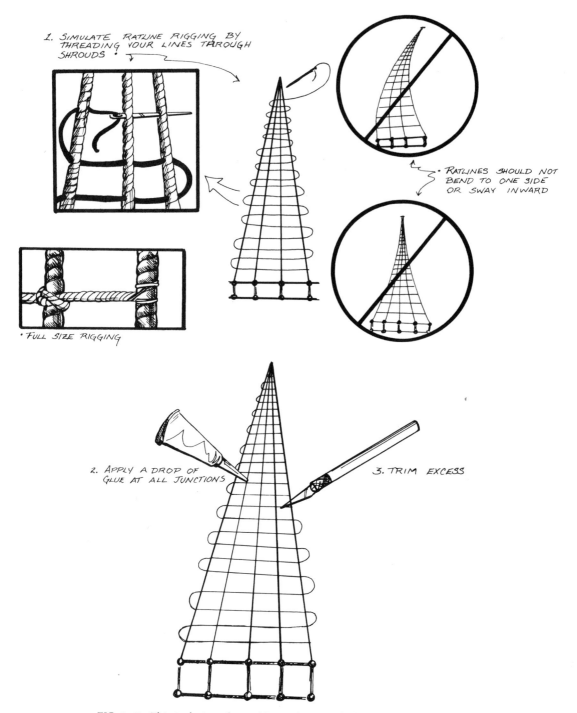

1. SIMULATE RATLINE RIGGING BY THREADING YOUR LINES THROUGH SHROUDS.

• FULL SIZE RIGGING

• RATLINES SHOULD NOT BEND TO ONE SIDE OR SWAY INWARD

2. APPLY A DROP OF GLUE AT ALL JUNCTIONS

3. TRIM EXCESS

FIG. 8–7   This technique for making ratlines is slightly more complicated than the procedure in Fig. 7–19, but it is more realistic. Be sure to trim off overhanging loops.

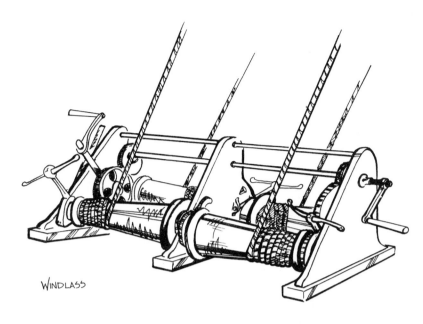

FIG. 8–8 Windlass rigging
can be turned onto the
drums and held secure with
a water thinned (50–50)
mixture of white glue.

WINDLASS

The stay is attached on the centerline of the ship fore of the mast it supports. The shrouds are attached just aft of the spar and as far to the sides (channels) as possible. If you visualize the completed shape, it forms a perfect three-dimensional pyramid, with the spar in the middle. The structure is very strong, suitable for keeping the spars upright in the strongest winds.

All rigging is subject to changes in weather conditions and humidity, and is therefore fully adjustable with tensioners. On older vessels, these are a system of deadeyes and lanyards, which are actually a common block and tackle. The lanyards are usually thinner, untreated rope. The strength comes in numbers rather than size. Modern ships, such as yachts and fishing vessels, use more efficient turnbuckles for the same purpose.

Shrouds on older ships usually carried the ratlines and were known to be "rattled down." Ratlines are usually thin rope, just heavy enough to support a man. On some more modern ships, these were replaced with wooden rungs.

Running rigging

A ship's running rigging handles a ship's running and operating gear. These are used to trim, hoist and lower the sails. You may

FIG. 8–9 Timberheads were usually ornate as well as practical.

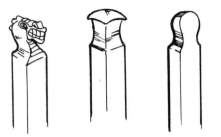

TIMBERHEADS - EXPOSED EDGES OF FRAME, CARVED FOR TYING ROPES TO.

FIG. 8–10 This illustration clearly shows the path of rigging on a typical block and tackle arrangement.

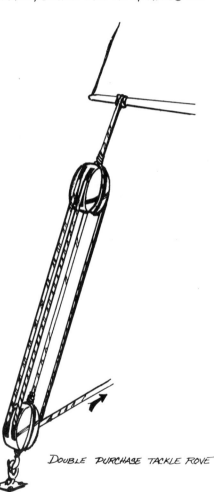

DOUBLE PURCHASE TACKLE ROVE

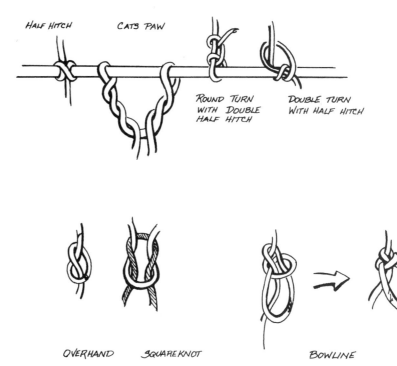

FIG. 8–11 *These are a few of the more common types of sailor's knots.*

want to consider how the model will be displayed at this point. Much of the running rigging is not used or even in place if the sails are stowed. Many modelers prefer to model a ship without sails because more detail can be seen. Additionally, it's difficult to make sails appear natural in scale. You have the problems of texture and heft which can't be scaled down easily. Conversely, you will miss out on much of the interesting running rigging detail if the model is displayed in a laid-up condition.

The most obvious components of the running rigging are the many different blocks and tackles used. The smaller eyes, hooks, etc. are usually too small to consider modeling. The same holds true for the hundreds of different knots a sailor was likely to know. The average modeler can get by with a few of the simpler, basic knots.

A few simple tools can vastly ease the problems of rigging in the smaller scales. A small fork can be fabricated out of wood, plastic or brass (Fig. 8-13), and used to guide the rigging lines. A

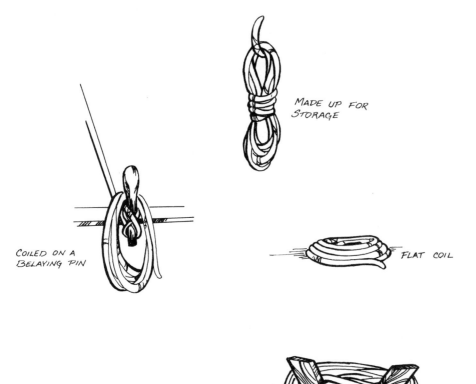

MADE UP FOR
STORAGE

COILED ON A
BELAYING PIN

FLAT COIL

COILED ON
A KEVEL

FIG. 8–12   Ropes are neatly
coiled in place. There is a
place for everything on a
well run ship.

FIG. 8–13   A homemade
fork will make rigging a lot
simpler than it would be
with tweezers or by hand.

RIGGING FORK- A PIECE OF BRASS
ROD HAMMERED FLAT AT ONE END
WITH A NOTCH CUT OUT.

THE MODEL SHIPBUILDING HANDBOOK

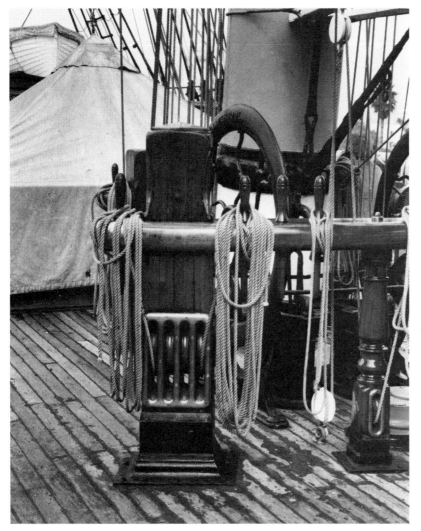

FIG. 8–14 The neatness of Star of India's rigging lends credence to the term "ship-shape."

FIG. 8–15 Plastic kit eye-bolts are not strong enough to use for rigging. Replace them with metal ones.

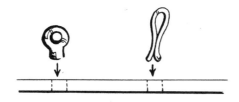

BRASS COTTER PINS CAN BE USED IN PLACE OF PLASTIC EYEBOLTS FOR ADDED STRENGTH

FIG. 8–16 Typical rigging
procedure.

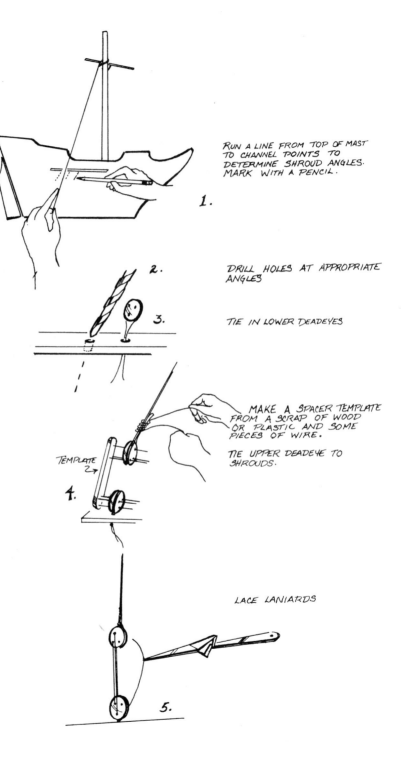

RUN A LINE FROM TOP OF MAST
TO CHANNEL POINTS TO
DETERMINE SHROUD ANGLES.
MARK WITH A PENCIL.

1.

2.

DRILL HOLES AT APPROPRIATE
ANGLES

3.

TIE IN LOWER DEADEYES

MAKE A SPACER TEMPLATE
FROM A SCRAP OF WOOD
OR PLASTIC AND SOME
PIECES OF WIRE.

TIE UPPER DEADEYE TO
SHROUDS.

TEMPLATE

4.

LACE LANIARDS

5.

112

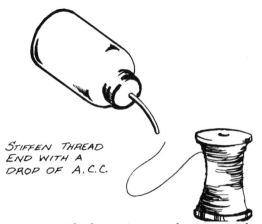

STIFFEN THREAD
END WITH A
DROP OF A.C.C.

pair of locking surgical tweezers with sharp tips are also essential. You may also want small surgical scissors to trim the lines once they're tied off. The best type are the ones used for cornea work. Hemostats are also handy for clamping or holding small items.

Real riggers almost always start at the front of the ship and work aft. This procedure would be advisable on a model as well, or you may find yourself tangled in a delicate web.

Thread specifically made for model ship-building is available from several suppliers through any good hobby shop. It is usually dyed a color appropriate for rope, although you may want to make it darker by soaking in strong tea or coffee. Thread is usually treated and is too stiff for use as is. It will not lay right or thread through the deadeyes easily unless you soak it in a fabric softener first.

You can create a "needle" at the tip of the thread by applying a drop of ACC (Hot Stuff) glue, to stiffen the end. Be sure to cut off this end after all of the lines are done.

FIG. 8–18 *Beeswax or clay can be as useful as an extra pair of hands while rigging.*

SMALL PIECES CAN BE
HELD WITH A LUMP OF
BEESWAX WHILE WORKING.

FIG. 8–19 Keep all lines taut but try to avoid bowing the masts.

Hold the thread up to a light; you will probably see dozens of wispy hairs hanging off. It may not be apparent to you now, but as the model ages and the thread gets greasy and dusty, these will stand out like a sore thumb. Draw the thread through a block of beeswax several times, then draw it through your fingers to

FIG. 8–20 Tying off rigging.

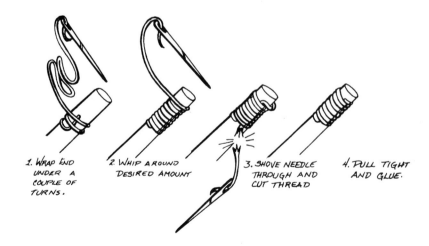

1. WRAP END UNDER A COUPLE OF TURNS.

2. WHIP AROUND DESIRED AMOUNT

3. SHOVE NEEDLE THROUGH AND CUT THREAD

4. PULL TIGHT AND GLUE.

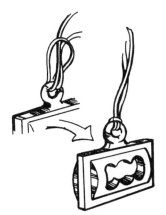

FIG. 8–21   It is always better visually to use realistic knots for all procedures whenever possible. Here are two methods for tying blocks to yards.

TYING BLOCKS TO YARDS

FIG. 8–22   A mouse was used frequently in place of a knot. It's not a difficult detail to duplicate.

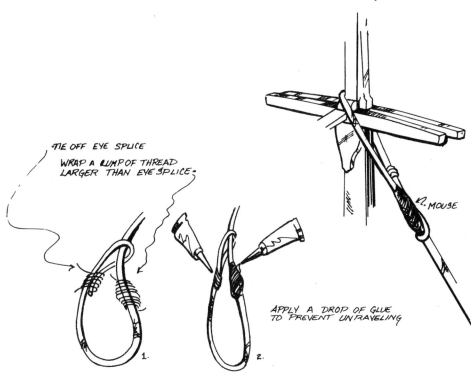

TIE OFF EYE SPLICE

WRAP A LUMP OF THREAD LARGER THAN EYE SPLICE.

APPLY A DROP OF GLUE TO PREVENT UNRAVELING

1.

2.

MOUSE

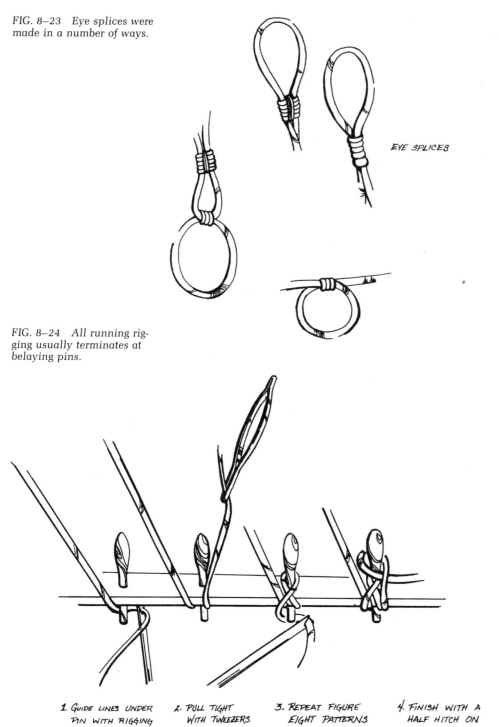

FIG. 8–23 Eye splices were made in a number of ways.

EYE SPLICES

FIG. 8–24 All running rigging usually terminates at belaying pins.

1. GUIDE LINES UNDER PIN WITH RIGGING FORK

2. PULL TIGHT WITH TWEEZERS

3. REPEAT FIGURE EIGHT PATTERNS

4. FINISH WITH A HALF HITCH ON LAST LOOP

FIG. 8–25 *Each line should
be tied off to its own belaying pin.*

scrape off any excess wax. Heat the thread over a light bulb to
impregnate the strands with soft wax. Finally, pass the thread
quickly over a candle flame to burn off any fine wisps that may
remain. At this point, the thread should hang fairly well and can
be pulled or stretched into position easily.

Try to apply a slight amount of tension on the lines as you
position and glue them in place so they will stay taut. Avoid
putting too much pressure on any one line, or it will bend the
masts or loosen other lines. I've used locking tweezers or surgical
forceps attached to the end of a line and allowed to hang free. The
weight of these is just enough to keep the lines taut. Apply thinned
white glue to the lines or apply ACC at the various juncture points.
Try to use real knots wherever possible. I've noticed that many
ship kits are simplified so much that the rigging lines terminate
at a deadeye and are glued in place, rather than tied off: the effect
is amateurish. Remember, extra effort in this area will produce a
more interesting model.

FIG. 8–26 This rope is tied off permanently for display. Note the fine rope to hold the larger rope.

All running lines should be tied off separately to a belaying pin or cleat, since they are frequently loosened or tightened. Standing rigging can be tied off to eyes with other lines; they are permanently installed.

PAINTING

9

Painting is the final step in a long chain of difficult operations. If you make a mistake at this stage, it can ruin the appearance of an otherwise perfect model. I've seen many models ruined by slip-shod work, such as a grainy finish, runs, and poor color choices. Conversely, I've seen some models that were masterpieces, but were nothing more than carefully finished stock kits. A good paint job can make even the lowly snap-kit look like it was made by a professional.

The material in most of this book has been set up like a cookbook. If you follow the steps in order, and save your creativity for later attempts, then you should get acceptable and pleasing results.

Throughout the rest of this chapter, we will be talking in a language new to some of you. The following are common terms you should learn.

Glossary of terms

BLEED.   The tinting of a top layer by a bottom coat of another color. Try spraying white over red! In a short while the white will turn pink. This is what is known as bleeding. The red bleeds through the white and tints it.

BLUSH.   Blushing is a milky fog effect on the surface of paint. It usually results from too much humidity in the air while painting.

BURNISH. To burnish is to make something shiny by buffing. Some paints and metals require burnishing or polishing for a smooth finish.

CRAZING. A rough or wrinkled effect is caused when a solvent such as lacquer thinner, liquid cement, or acetone is applied to plastic. It can be desirable for simulating cloth. Plastic model sails can be sprayed or brushed with acetone and the wrinkle effect will simulate canvas. Lacquers will also do this to plastics if sprayed directly without first sealing the plastic with a surface primer.

ENAMEL. Enamel is the paint most commonly used. It is a slow drying paint containing color pigments suspended in varnish. Solvent in enamel evaporates much like lacquer, but the pigments tend to settle out and the glossy varnish starts to cure. It takes enamel quite a long time to dry. The surface may feel dry to touch but the undersurface takes quite a bit longer to really harden. Enamel is desirable for brushing because of its slow drying time. If applied properly, enamel will yield a surface that is virtually chip resistant. Lacquer is brittle and will chip.

FLASH. Flash is when paint dries too quickly. Lacquers often flash-dry, leaving a dull, rough surface.

FLOW. The flow of paint is the way it covers a surface. Flow can be altered by changing the type of solvent, especially in lacquers. In increased humidity, lacquer will take longer to flow out. When brushed, enamels flow out much better than lacquers.

HUE. The color of the finish coat. It is not the brightness of the paint.

LACQUER. Lacquer is a fast-drying, sweet-smelling paint that is used when quick, dust-free paint jobs are desired. Lacquer has either a nitrocellulose or acrylic plastic base. Acetone dissolves lacquer but is also a plastic solvent. For this reason, straight lacquer should not be used directly on plastic unless a special wrinkled effect is desired. Several good lacquers which will not cause crazing are now available for plastic.

Lacquer hardens when the solvent evaporates, so lacquer can be used when time is a limiting factor. Lacquer has to be rubbed to make it glossy, whereas enamel does not. Lacquer has a "sheen" while enamel has a "shine." When you paint with lacquer you are less likely to have runs than with slower drying enamel. Lacquer is a poor brush paint, as it sets up quickly and dries too fast for good flow.

METALLIC.   Metallic paint has minute particles of aluminum, gold, bronze, or some other powder mixed into the solution. It reflects light in such a manner as to give a metal-like finish. Metallic bronze is good for clad hulls.

ORANGE PEEL.   A rough dimpled effect caused by improper paint flow or too much air pressure. The surface resembles the surface of an orange.

OVERSPRAY.   Paint dust created by paint which does not land on the object being painted. If you've been around a paint shop you'll notice that the floor, furniture, and so on, will often have overspray dust on them.

PIGMENT.   Small particles of solid colored material added to solvent to give paint the desired color.

PRIMER.   Primer is often used to describe both primer and primer/surfacer. Primer is a very heavy enamel which dries flat. It is specially formulated to adhere to surfaces to form an underbase for enamel paint. A primer/surfacer is mostly lacquer, which will seal plastic so that any kind of lacquer finish may be used. Primer/surfacer sands beautifully and is extremely valuable for a top-quality show finish.

RUBBING COMPOUND.   An oily liquid or paste that is used in polishing (rubbing out) lacquer paint. Rubbing compound "cuts" the paint surface just as an extremely fine sandpaper would. Toothpaste can be used as rubbing compound for a fine finish.

RUN.   A problem caused by applying too much paint in one spot. The weight of paint causes it to flow downward when painting a flat surface. A run that is only slightly noticeable is called a sag.

TACK RAG.   A sticky cloth used by professional painters to remove dust prior to painting.

TONE.   The brilliance and intensity of the paint.

UNDERCOAT.   The first layer of paint, usually a primer.

VARNISH.   A preparation made of resin dissolved in oil or in a liquid, such as alcohol. It dries to a high gloss or satin finish and is used on wood surfaces. Varnish is the vehicle in enamel which takes such a long time to cure properly.

VEHICLE.   The paint pigment carrier. In enamel, varnish is known as the vehicle.

WAX.   There are many waxes on the market, which are suitable for use on models. Some waxes contain silicones which can cause trouble if you plan to repaint the model. Blue Coral doesn't contain silicone and can be used after carefully compounding the lacquer. Blue Coral Sealer can be used on enamels shortly after painting, but most automotive waxes cannot. For lacquer, you can obtain a much higher gloss using something like DuPont New Car Wax after a suitable drying time. Wax helps keep greasy fingers and dust scratches from damaging the surface of a fine model.

WET SANDING.   Wet-and-dry sandpapers can be used with water. These papers are especially desirable because the flow of water keeps the paper from clogging and acts as a lubricant. You can use wet sandpaper to smooth out a lacquer finish. Wet-sanding obtains the desired results much quicker than dry on plastic because of the faster cutting of clean paper.

Paint types

Most spray paints available to the modeler are found in aerosol cans, which use air or a propellant to drive out the paint. There is usually a small steel ball which keeps the pigment mixed with the solvent.

By heating the can in water before painting, you will increase the pressure on the can, thus making a finer spray. Using common tap water you can be assured that the can will not explode, unless the tap water is excessively hot (over 150 degrees). The warm paint also will have better flow characteristics.

OPAQUE.   Solid, non-metallic reds, blues, greens, blacks, whites, etc., are examples of the opaques. Opaques will cover a plastic surface in two coats. These are available in both lacquer and enamel.

Preparation

A lot of modelers believe that their biggest problem is when the paint is applied, but the "secret" to beautiful painting is not in the application but in preparation.

Dust and runs are the biggest enemies in model painting. Runs

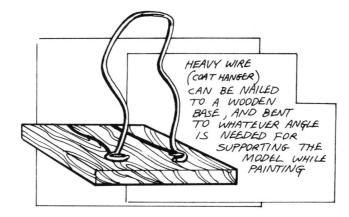

HEAVY WIRE
(COAT HANGER)
CAN BE NAILED
TO A WOODEN
BASE, AND BENT
TO WHATEVER ANGLE
IS NEEDED FOR
SUPPORTING THE
MODEL WHILE
PAINTING

FIG. 9–1 A stand should be made to support the model while painting.

can be eliminated for the most part by the use of lacquers. Dust on the other hand is a problem for the best of painters.

Paint stands are necessary to keep fingerprints and dust particles out of the paint. These stands should be made out of a coat hanger before you are ready to paint. Holding the model in your hand while painting is the poorest technique you can use. You are likely to spray your fingers, and also leave oily fingerprints on the plastic.

If the ship isn't equipped with a stand (such as Aurora's), cut a round hole in the bottom of the hull to take a stand made of coat hanger wire. An X-Acto knife twisted in a circle works well. The coat hanger should be shaped so that it will go up through the hole, yet support the model when placed in the box. The base of the stand should extend beyond the back of the model and be counterbalanced for its weight.

Prior to painting, take time to set up a spray booth with a fan to draw out the excess paint fumes through a filter. If you're going to build a lot of models, it will keep the workroom free of paint dust, and improve your quality.

Spray cans should be warmed for 60 seconds in warm (not hot) water.

When all putty work is completed, sand the entire model with #400 wet-and-dry sandpaper. Lightly wash the model. Dry it thoroughly with a lint-free cloth or hair dryer.

Apply a coat of primer to the model. It will show up rough spots not noticed after the preliminary sanding. Pits or cracks should be filled with putty and wet-sanded smooth with #400 wet-and-dry sandpaper.

FIG. 9–2 If the model is very rough, it will help to alternate between different colors of primer. This way you will see where low and high spots still need work.

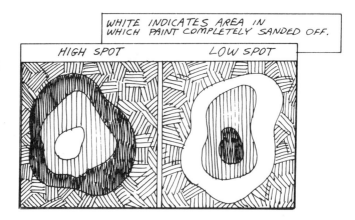

Clean the model, prime and recheck for bad spots. Apply a couple more coats of primer and allow them to dry for about eight hours. Using two primer colors will help highlight problem areas.

Wet-sand the model lightly with #600 wet-and-dry paper. Be careful not to sand through the primer coats.

Weather is one of the most important factors to consider when painting. Never try painting when it is raining or extremely damp; too much water vapor in the air affects the paint, causing it to blush. Extremely hot weather causes lacquer to fog or cloud, and dry too quickly, resulting in a dull finish. The best paint jobs are achieved when the temperature is between 65 to 78 degrees.

Brush painting

I paint all my detail with a regular brush. It requires no elaborate equipment or time-consuming masking.

Select the right kind of paint for brush painting. Not all paints are suitable for plastic models, and not all paints are suitable for brush painting. At this time, the best brushing paints available are Pactra "Namel" or Humbrol paints. Testor's paints dry too quickly.

After purchasing the colors you need, avoid shaking the bottles. Instead, unscrew the top, pour out and discard the oil which has accumulated on top of the paint. Now stir the remaining paint in the jar very thoroughly. If this procedure is not followed, the first coat of paint will be too transparent and another coat will be needed. Not only does a second coat of paint hide fine detail, but there is an increased chance of error. A good brush job should be achieved with one coat of paint only. A brush is a tool, and if properly handled, even a cheap brush will give satisfactory results. For large surfaces, a brush of medium (¼″) width is enough. A very wide brush is usually a handicap. For small parts, choose small brushes to your taste. For a striping job, use the smallest brush available (10 "nought").

Spray booth

Most people have problems with spray painting. Wet paint picks up enough dust and lint to ruin a perfect paint job. In addition most paint fumes are toxic and constitute a fire hazard. I've solved both of these problems by constructing a portable benchtop spray booth. (Refer to *The Model-Building Handbook* published by Chilton for full construction details.)

Airbrushing

I have very strong feelings about painting since it is such an important aspect of modeling. There is no substitute for an airbrushed paint job. The airbrush acts like a miniature, scaled-down version of a real spray gun. Air rushes past an orifice and atomizes a controlled flow of paint to produce a fine mist. The airbrush gives the added advantage of being able to mix any color and control the width of the spray. A good painter can produce a fine line or blend from one color to another, techniques which are impossible with a can or brush.

You may feel that a spray can gives satisfactory results and that the added expense is not really necessary. You may be right for the circumstances of your modeling. However, if you are concerned with achieving the best possible finish or if you're a professional, by all means get an airbrush and compressor. The expense should be considered an investment.

Airbrushes are sold in virtually all hobby shops and are marketed by a number of companies. I am most familiar with the Paasche, Binks, and Thayer and Chandler.

You will also need a steady supply of air. The source can be something as cheap and simple as an inner tube with a special attachment, or an aerosol can. There are a number of single-stage compressors on the market for less than $100, but they don't have

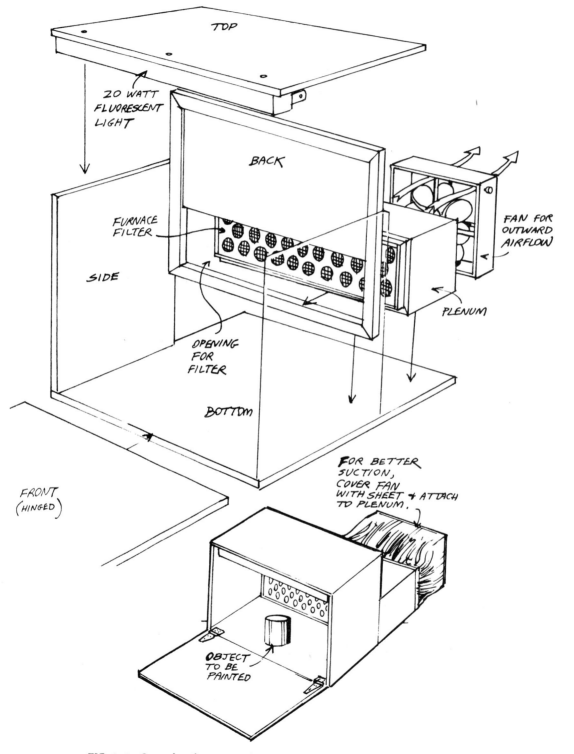

FIG. 9–3 Spray booth construction.

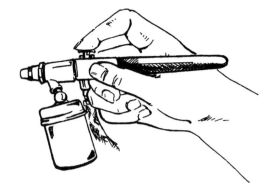

FIG. 9–4 *You will have better control over an air-brush if it is held like a pen.*

any means of regulation and the air often comes out in pulses. A large compressor with storage tank and adjustable pressure release may be cumbersome for the average modeler, but it is a good investment and often can be used elsewhere in the house.

Paint must be fresh, clean and free of lumps. Any foreign matter will cause the airbrush to clog and cause endless problems. Strain all paint through an old pair of nylons or cheesecloth. You'll be amazed at the junk left behind!

Paint should be thinned for airbrushing, because the air rushing by the nozzle tends to dry out the mixture, making the paint thicker and drier by the time it reaches the model. This rapid drying is one of the airbrush's advantages and selling points. Lacquers can be used straight on plastic because the solvents dry so quickly, not allowing time for them to attack the surface. The proper ratio for most paints is in the range of 30 to 50 percent thinner to paint. The amount depends on atmospheric conditions, personal taste, type of paint and type of airbrush. Experiment with various ratios prior to painting the model. Too much thinner can affect the stickiness and flow-out characteristics of the paint.

The work area must be well-ventilated and free of dust. You may want to build a spray booth as mentioned earlier in this book.

A single-action airbrush should be held in one hand with the index finger over the actuator button. The other hand can be used to control flow at the adjusting knob. This type of unit is a little simpler to use, but it does not have the immediate, finite control of the dual-action units.

Hold a dual-action unit the same way, but remember: pulling back on the trigger also controls paint flow. This extremely handy feature allows you to easily vary line width or blend colors. You

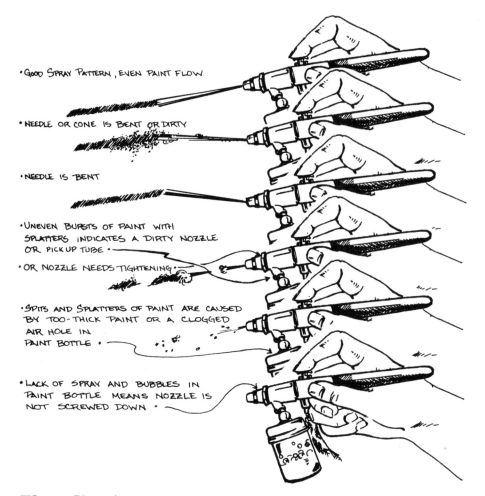

• GOOD SPRAY PATTERN, EVEN PAINT FLOW

• NEEDLE OR CONE IS BENT OR DIRTY

• NEEDLE IS BENT

• UNEVEN BURSTS OF PAINT WITH SPLATTERS INDICATES A DIRTY NOZZLE OR PICK UP TUBE •

• OR NOZZLE NEEDS TIGHTENING •

• SPITS AND SPLATTERS OF PAINT ARE CAUSED BY TOO-THICK PAINT OR A CLOGGED AIR HOLE IN PAINT BOTTLE •

• LACK OF SPRAY AND BUBBLES IN PAINT BOTTLE MEANS NOZZLE IS NOT SCREWED DOWN •

FIG. 9–5 *Diagnosing a problem with an airbrush is easy if you know what to look for. Each problem has a unique set of symptoms.*

can also use the pull-back feature to clear the unit if it temporarily clogs.

The final coat of paint should be wet with a considerable amount of thinner sprayed from very close. Some modelers even use straight thinner to draw out the varnish and produce a smooth glossy finish. Experiment on scrap first.

If you are using aerosol cans as a propellant, you may find that they appear to run out quickly when used for long stretches of time. In fact, they will revive if allowed to return to room temperature slowly.

Clean the airbrush immediately after each use by running

thinner through instead of paint. Remove the needle and wipe it off. Clean out the jar or cup thoroughly. Chips of dry paint could ruin later paint jobs. You may have to take the entire unit apart occasionally if it starts to act up. Follow the manufacturer's instructions.

Rubbing compound

Rubbing compound brings out the luster in lacquer and plastic when the surfaces are polished. Since most models are small, you can't be too sloppy in your technique. You'll need a soft rag such as an old T-shirt or diaper. To hold a polishing cloth correctly, lay out the cloth, push your index finger into the middle, and then flip the rag over your finger. Twist the top of the rag so that it pulls tightly around the tip of your finger. Tuck the twist and excess back into your hand and you are ready to use the compound.

Apply the compound to an area about 2 inches square. Rub back and forth with firm but not hard strokes. Occasionally wet the rag with a small cup of water to keep the compound oil working out evenly. Color on the rag shows that the compound is cutting. The first few strokes require more pressure than the final polishing ones.

As the polished shine starts to appear, ease up on the pressure and start lightly buffing. Use a clean damp area on the rag with no compound. Buff the paint until you get a brilliant gloss.

Striping, lettering, decals

The "make it or break it" time in model-building is when it comes time to paint and detail. This is where the average model builder usually gets stage fright. Yet, detailing is probably the greatest source of satisfaction you will find, if it's done right. You can create excellent models if you follow just a few simple rules and use the right equipment for the job.

Stripes

Stripes are probably the easiest step toward realistic detailing. They can be painted or applied with adhesive material. Both methods are simple and effective. The kind of detailing usually dictates the method. If the model is an injection-molded plastic piece, such as Monogram's or Revell's, mask the area you want to stripe, and flow on a thin coat of paint with a #1 brush. Use regular automotive masking tape. Before the paint gets too tacky, lift the tape off in one smooth motion.

If you paint too thickly, you will find there are edges built up along both sides of the stripe. These are very difficult to smooth out, and care should be taken to prevent this problem. When the paint is thoroughly dry, use rubbing compound to smooth out the edges.

An easier method is to use the stripes from a decal set. Lay a ruler along the stripe and cut it from the decal sheet with an X-Acto knife. Stay close to the actual decal so you get as little of the "lip" or edge, which surrounds every decal. Wet the stripe until it slides from its backing and slide it onto the model. Pat it dry with an absorbent piece of cloth, or cotton. Once it begins to dry, don't attempt to move it; you will only succeed in tearing it.

A decal strip works well for the outside of a plastic body because it is very thin and will not project above the surface of the shell too far. However, this is not the case with striping tape.

FIG. 9–6 *This boat was highlighted with rub-on letters and striping tape.*

This tape, although very popular, usually sticks up like a "sore thumb." If you use it, shop around until you find the thinnest tape available. It has an adhesive backing and is easily applied.

Another way to put stripes on your model is with sheets of extremely thin acetate with lines printed on it, which many art stores carry. The printed material is as thin as paint and can easily be transferred by rubbing. There are many different trade names; the one I use the most is Letraset. Check with your local dealer for available brands. All you have to do is cut the stripe from the sheet and press it in place. Presto, instant stripes!

Lettering

A first class job of hand-lettering will set your model apart from any group. Decals are fine, but when you can't find the right decal for the job, try paint!

Hand-lettering requires good, quality brushes. The best brushes come from West Germany, and most hobby shops do carry them. Don't buy a cheap brush! I can't stress this too strongly! A good brush will last for years, and the few cents difference in original cost is negligible. There's nothing more discouraging than a paint-brush that starts to lose hair in the middle of a job. The four sizes you will need are #1, #0, #00, and #000. The #1 is the largest and #000 is the smallest with a real "needle point" for extremely fine work.

I prefer a good, free-flowing enamel for hand-lettering, such as Testor's PLA enamels. Never dip a brush down into a bottle. You usually dip it too far, because you can't see what you're doing. Before starting to paint, tip the bottle upside down, then set upright and remove the lid. There is usually just the right amount of paint left in the lid for hand-lettering. If it needs thinning, add a drop or two of Testor's thinner in the cap and mix evenly.

Pass the brush through the paint with the handle angled sharply. Roll the brush in your hand so the point looks "wet" and has a sharp point. The paint should flow smoothly from your brush. When it stops flowing, stop painting and dip the brush again. You can't "brush out" paint when lettering. Avoid a "build up" of paint, which is caused by too much paint flowing from the brush. Practice will really pay off!

It's a good idea to lightly pencil in the lettering, before you begin to paint. Guide lines are very important.

Always clean the brush thoroughly after using. It will keep the bristles fresh and pliable for a long time.

Decals

You can purchase decals with almost any design in manufacturer's trademarks, plus a variety of numbers, fields, and stripes. They are easy to apply, and even a novice can do a good job the first time.

Trim excess material away around the decal. Soak the decal in warm water, and it should separate from the backing material within 30 seconds. Slide it onto the surface of the model and position it while it is still wet. Blot dry with an absorbent cloth.

When the decals are dry, spray the entire model with Testor's Chip Guard or Floquil Clear Coat. These will seal the decals and paint to prevent chipping and scratching.

Clear coat

Spraying a coat of paint that adds no color may seem a bit illogical, but you do see more than just colors—there is also texture.

A clear coating, applied over the final paint and decals, can dull the unsightly shine of an airplane model, or hide the edges of decals, or make many brush-painted finishes look as though they were spray-painted by a professional. Clear paints can also simplify the job by allowing you to use high-gloss (shiny) enamels, with their accompanying range of color selection and ease of application, for any painted surface.

Decals will stick better to a glossy surface than a dull one, conforming closer to the contours of the surface of the model. If you desire a flat (no gloss) finish, a final spray coat of clear flat paint like Testor's Dullcote should be applied after the decals are in place. On many models, the plastic may be the color you wish to retain, but you aren't satisfied with the "plastic look" of the model. Flat clear paint can make the texture appear to be more lifelike.

Model structure kits like buildings, etc., will seem more realistic when sprayed with Dullcote to give the appearance of a building weathered by the sun and rain.

Clear paint is also excellent protection for the finish of a model. Both paint and decals will stand more handling when they are protected.

Dullcote and Glosscote are brand names for dull or gloss, clear, lacquer-based paint. They can be safely applied over almost any paint or plastic. However, try each out on a scrap of the paint or plastic to be coated before spraying the completed model, to be certain the surface won't be damaged. You may use a generic brand to save some money or for use with an airbrush, but be sure to test the paint first.

As with most spray paints, the finish will be smoother if both model and paint are at room temperature. Obviously, the model and spray area should be dust-free as well.

Clear gross paint will produce the highest gloss and the smoothest finish if sprayed from 10 to 12 inches from the model in smooth, even strokes, starting the spray just off the edge of the model and swinging the can at a consistant rate across the model's surface. It is difficult to tell how much clear paint is applied because there is no color change; to prevent runs and sags, spray on two or more thin coats.

Dull paint produces the least gloss and the flattest finish if it is held about 18 to 24 inches from the model. Its spray, too, should be started off to one side of the model and consistently moved across the surface. Several coats of Dullcote are best, with each coat quickly "dusted" over the model and allowed to dry before the next coat.

Removing paint from plastic

A toothbrush and Cox Thimble-Drome Glow Fuel or K & B Fuel are all the equipment you need to remove paint from a plastic body. These fuels will not "craze" plastic but will remove most paint. There are some new commercial products, available at model train shops, which reportedly remove paint from plastic as well. Dip the toothbrush into the fuel and brush it on briskly. The fuel will take one to two hours to soften the paint.

For best results, rub in the direction of scribe lines and contour lines. After paint has been removed, scrub the model with warm, soapy water to remove all residue. Be sure to rinse thoroughly with clear water.

SUPER-DETAILING

10

Careful attention to small details can add immeasureably to the appearance and realism of a model ship, setting it apart from others of the same type. The technique can be something as basic as adding a thin wash of black paint to the metal plates on a hull or as complex as a sunken ship. It's the small touches which apparently go unnoticed that add the greatest sense of reality. I always add little details to our movie models, which I know will not register on the conscious mind of an observer but will add to the illusion.

Let's suppose that you are making a detailed replica of a wharf scene with a ship at anchor. The average modeler will paint the boat some dirty color, stain the wharf and create "water" out of resin and let it go at that. The better modeler will airbrush some streaks on the ship and wharf and add a few scattered figures. The super-detailer will take the time to research what a real wharf might look like. The details would include heavy weathering, dents on the ship, an old drunk sleeping near a building, scraps of paper and other debris, rats on the ropes leading to the ship, a small light on the gang plank (even if it is day), barnacles on the pilings, puddles, et cetera. The possibilities are endless. Take time to think about what you are trying to portray and many clever details will come to mind. It can be extended to the display around the model; I love creating tiny vignettes to go with my display models.

FIG. 10–1   *Note the details of barnacles, scars, and rust.*

Black wash

A wash of thin, runny, flat black paint can do wonders on virtually any model. It is the quickest and cheapest of tricks. I use either enamel or Polly-S water soluble paints. The latter can be controlled well, does not eat away the base paint, and can be washed off if the results are less than perfect. You may prefer to use watercolors because they can be washed off, unless a clear coat is applied for protection.

A good starting mixture is half paint and half thinner. Fill a fairly large brush with the mix and brush it over the surface. Allow the paint to nearly dry and gently wipe off highlights with a soft cloth. The black left in the recesses will emphasize the dimensionality of the piece. The same technique can be used to accent door or panel scribe lines. I use this technique frequently, and it yields an amazing sense of realism for very little effort.

FIG. 10–2 *Rust and soot appear on even a fastidiously kept ship.*

Scrap box

Keep any spare parts left from a kit-building project. I haven't thrown away anything for years. You'll always find a use for something. Dioramas beg for little details such as trash cans, crates, et cetera. Litter is prevalent everywhere in real life. Observe how

your own neighborhood or a fishing pier looks sometime, and try to capture that feeling.

Flags

Every ship, regardless of the size, requires flags of several types and sizes. The average modeler may have the ability to create flags from scratch, but I would strongly advise against it because of the many ready-made flags available.

If you must make your own flags, research them very carefully. Flags change frequently; our own flag has been in three different configurations in the last three decades.

Most kits come with flags printed on paper. These can be made to look better by wetting, crumpling, and weathering, but

FIG. 10–5 This builder used model airplane kits to outfit his ship.

you would do better switching to cloth. Cloth flags can be made to hang nicely by soaking them in fabric softener.

Scratchbuilt flags can be made using fine linen and marking pens designed specifically for fabric. These pens contain ink which won't bleed. You may also use acrylics or oil paints. Work slowly and try not to get the material too wet, or the color will bleed. Use double-sided tape to hold the cloth flat while you're painting it.

Weathering

As a different approach to modeling, weathering can produce an interesting and very realistic looking piece. Although weathering can make any model look authentic, too much or the wrong technique can ruin it.

FIG. 10–6 *Note the string of parts trees behind the modeler, which are a source of random detail parts.*

The first step in weathering a model is to observe the actual object. Look for worn paint, fuel spillage, salt spray, minor dents, or anything that adds to that "used" look. If you can, watch the ships in action. Try to see how the dirt and water gets where it is. Take pictures to help you remember details. If you are using black and white film, make mental notes about the color of rust, or salt spray.

The materials needed to weather a model are 1. an airbrush (a spray can will do in a pinch); 2. a piece of cardboard, 12 by 18 inches; 3. various colors of flat bottle paint: grays for grime, brown and tan for dirt or salt spray, black for fuel or oil spills and soot, and oranges for rust; and small and medium-size brushes. When buying paint, be sure to get brands that blend together without separating.

FIG. 10–7 Keep a file of
real-life photos, to use as a
guide in weathering your
model.

The first step is to mix paint for the overall salt spray or dust. In a covered container, mix one and one half parts thinner to one part paint and lightly shake the bottle. Pour it in an airbrush bottle and test it on a piece of scrap. Hold the airbrush about 12 to 15 inches from the work, and make one or two light passes. If the solution is too thin, add more paint; if it's too thick, add more thinner. Keep practicing until you have the solution right and have gained the feeling of the airbrush. A couple of light passes should be sufficient.

Position the cardboard halfway down the side of the model, so the bulk of the spray hits the bottom half of the hull. Do all sides, with just one pass for each. Then lift the cardboard and

FIG. 10–8 *Weathering can be done with an airbrush or with thin water-based paints.*

spray the entire model lightly. Be careful, if you over-do it, the effect might be ruined.

Graffiti scratched on the back of a fishing boat where dirt build-up is the heaviest lends realism. It can be accomplished by scratching off the tan paint with a fine wire, allowing the aluminum undercoat to show through. Dimestore necklace chains can be used to simulate heavy chains. Diesel fuel and hydraulic fluid spills can be made by thinning flat black paint and dribbling the mixture down the side of the model with a brush.

Be sure to add splash marks on exposed surfaces with the dry brush technique. Dip the brush in the desired color and blot it on newspaper a couple of times. Then, with a few quick strokes, apply lightly to the surface. Repeat until the desired area is covered.

When you paint a metal ship model, begin with a coat of aluminum or rust-colored paint. Let dry, then apply the desired top color. After the top layer of paint has dried, rub lightly with fine rubbing compound until the lower layer shows through. The

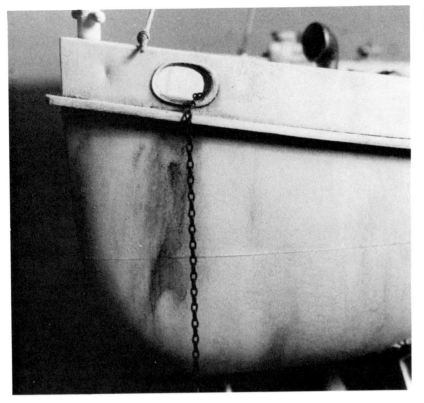

FIG. 10–9 Chains can be purchased or scratchbuilt.

end result will look as though paint has worn down to the metal in areas where rope or chain has abraded.

Minor dents can be made by heating any blunt metal object and pressing it on the desired area. Try not to melt the plastic, just soften it.

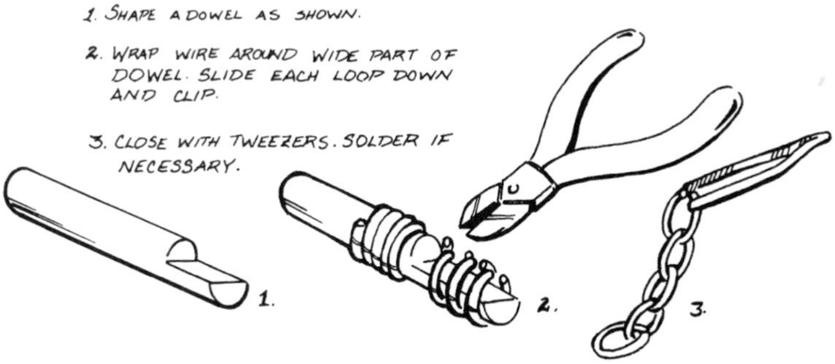

1. SHAPE A DOWEL AS SHOWN.

2. WRAP WIRE AROUND WIDE PART OF DOWEL. SLIDE EACH LOOP DOWN AND CLIP.

3. CLOSE WITH TWEEZERS. SOLDER IF NECESSARY.

1. 2. 3.

FIG. 10–10 Chains of odd sizes can be made using wire if a size you need is not available.

SUPER-DETAILING
143

FIG. 10–11 Scuff the hull
to expose primer and to
simulate rusty metal.

Smoke or soot can be made with an airbrush filled with flat
black paint. Lightly spray exhaust stack tips, and areas that are
near exhaust stacks.

Lighting

Lighting can create a fine display item and add a great deal of life
to any display.

Grain-of-wheat and grain-of-rice bulbs are good sources of
point light, but an extra dimension is lent to any smaller scale
model through the use of fiber optics. These fibers are made from
glass or plastic. The latter are better for model work for several
reasons: safety (no glass shards) and the ability to use regular
plastic adhesives (since they are styrene). They can be found in
several sizes, but kits for fiber optic lamps carry fibers of good
average diameter and possess advantages over loose fibers.

FIG. 10–12 *Lights make a model look more realistic.*

All the fibers in the kit are tied together at one end with a metal collar, saving you untold hassle. The kit also comes with a base that can be used for your model, into which the collared end of the fibers fits directly, providing a tightly controlled housing for the light source. Another advantage of fiber optics is one light for the entire model.

When planning the placement of lighting in the model, be sure the collared end is mounted somewhere near the center so all the fibers will reach the holes you must drill for them.

Select a fine drill bit which will make a hole just slightly larger than the fiber. (The model should not be assembled at this point since the fibers are run through the body). When all the holes are drilled, begin "threading' each with a fiber, going from the interior of the model to exterior.

To keep the fiber from sliding back through the hole, a process called lensing must be applied to the end of each fiber. Using a soldering pencil, lightly touch the flat tip of the fiber to any hot

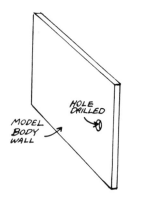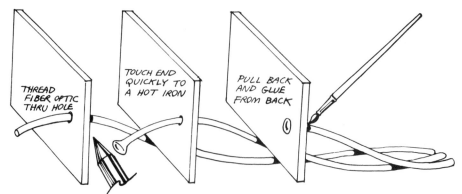

MODEL BODY WALL — HOLE DRILLED

THREAD FIBER OPTIC THRU HOLE

TOUCH END QUICKLY TO A HOT IRON

PULL BACK AND GLUE FROM BACK

FIG. 10–13   Fiber optics are a simple and easy way to add lighting effects to a model.

section of the metal. The end of the fiber will flare out in the shape of a small lens. Do this very quickly or the fiber will flare too much and melt. A candle can be used if a soldering pencil is not available, but practice with some spare fibers until you can repeat good results.

If any of the fibers must bend tightly to emerge from a hole, a hair dryer applied to the area of the abrupt angle will softly bend the fiber. Fibers transmit light through a plastic core which is surrounded by another plastic sheath. As long as there are no actual "kinks" in a bend, it will still deliver all the light from the source. Check the fibers carefully before insertion.

Rivets

For years I had tried to locate a simple, inexpensive rivet machine. One day, while killing time in a sewing shop, I noticed a gadget hanging on a rack that looked like a pizza cutter with teeth. The display card showed the device in use copying patterns onto material by punching holes through the paper and leaving chalk marks on the fabric.

My first attempts yielded ugly, uneven holes in thin sheet brass and thin sheet plastic. But after many experiments with material thickness, I finally got it, and it was a snap!

Any sewing shop should carry one or more styles of the pattern-tracing wheels. I've since discovered that there is more than one manufacturer of these things and that the spacing varies from make to make. Three such wheels can yield an infinite array of rivets for use in any scale.

The second item you'll need is a fairly large (one foot square)

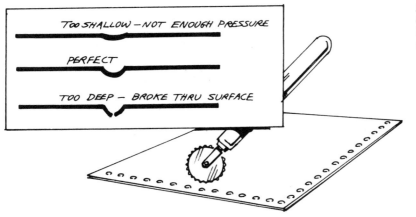

FIG. 10–14 Rivets can be embossed into plastic or brass shim stock using a seamstress' wheel.

piece of hard, flat, smooth rubber. I found mine in a war surplus store. A piece of hardwood will work fairly well. This hard, but giving surface is necessary to develop evenly shaped rivets. If the surface is too hard, the rivets won't form at all. Too soft, and the wheel will punch through.

The best method for producing rivets on most models is to fabricate a skin or rivet strips. The tool cannot form rivets in material thicker than .020 inch, but this is too thin for most models. The best rivets are formed in the thinnest material, .010 inch thick.

Rivets are best made when the plastic or metal is pliable and not brittle. Warm the plastic under hot tap water for a few minutes to soften it.

Determine where the rivets are to go and mark their location with a soft pencil. These marks will wash off in warm soapy water later when the model is finished.

Practice on a scrap piece of plastic prior to trying this on the model. Use a straightedge to guide the punch on straight segments. Free-handing is difficult, even with a steady hand. Some minor lack of uniformity is desirable for realism, but don't get carried away. Real rivets may be off by a full inch at worst, which should be divided by whatever scale you're working in. Try different degrees of pressure to decide what looks best for the model you're building. Light pressure will yield small, poorly defined rivets suitable for very small scale models or small rivet heads. Heavy pressure, just under what would form a hole, is usually the best. Don't worry if the tip punches slightly through the material. Paint will fill these spots when the model is finished.

FIG. 10–15 Metal ships are covered with rivets, which are easy to simulate, with the proper tool.

If the stock spacing of the rivets isn't suitable, carefully position the tool with a tooth between two adjacent rivets. Guide the tool slowly and carefully to avoid punching one rivet onto another. A safer method is to have a second row of rivets just above the first row, with the new rivets spaced unevenly with the first row.

Free-handing curving rows of rivets is acceptable if you have a carefully drawn guideline. However, you can achieve excellent results using a French curve instead.

A rivet-covered plastic skin can be glued to the model using a drop of liquid cement in the center of the piece to be fitted. A small drop of glue also applied in each corner will assure a firm, even bond. Too much glue will ruin the plastic.

A brass rivet-covered skin can be "sweat-soldered" in place or soldered along the edges to the base of the model.

1. APPLY GLUE TO BOTH SURFACES

3. WEIGHT DOWN ALL EDGES AND ALLOW TO DRY.

2. WHEN TACKY, START APPLYING VENEER FROM ONE EDGE, ROLLING OUT AIR BUBBLES WITH A HARD RUBBER BREYER.

FIG. 10–16 Veneer can be laminated to create real wood trim.

I've used this rivet method for many models and find it to be easy and rewarding. I've built models that would have been impossible to build otherwise, without sacrificing some detail. It takes a little practice and experimentation, but the effect is well worth it.

Real wood trim

Would you like to have real wood as thin as paper; wood you can cut with a pair of scissors or an X-Acto knife! Imagine how it would simplify decking or planking. Flexwood is a real wood product that's only 1/86 inch thick (just a shade thicker than the paper this book is printed on). There are two types—architectural Flexwood (with a cloth backing), and designer Flexwood, which is paper-backed. The latter appears to be better-suited to model applications.

The following woods are currently available; ash, avodire, benge birch, butternut, American cherry, wormy chestnut, elm, macassar ebony, fir, red gum, koa, korina, lacewood, African mahogany, Honduras mahogany, makori, maple, narra, red oak, white oak, English brown oak, orientalwood, paldao, knotty pine, prima vera, redwood burl, rosewood, sapeli, satinwood, teak, tigerwood, American walnut, claro walnut, and zebrawood.

The flat-cut type is most like the wood used on a ship. Use Ambroid or white glue for installing this material on wood parts, or contact cement (Weldwood or Pliobond) for attachment to metal or plastic. Any clear varnish, lacquer, or dope (fuel-proof varnish) could be used as a final gloss finish.

FIGURES

11

Large ship models such as the Cutty Sark or Constitution, though impressive, unfortunately can't do justice to the awesome size of these vessels. Adding human figures gives life and drama to the model, while giving a scale size that is easily recognized.

Painting, creating, or modifying figures for a ship model can be a fascinating, frustrating, educational, and thoroughly engrossing hobby in itself. The procedures and skills required are not too difficult for the average person.

Most of these techniques described here can be applied to the entire model. Objects offen suffer from a sort of flat appearance. Highlighting and shading give my models a natural, organic look.

The first rule to remember is that nature abhors solid, shiny colors and pristine items. Anything that isn't brand new will show signs of wear, deterioration, and weathering. Therefore, if you have just painted a sailor with glossy baby blue paint and wonder why it doesn't look right, now you know.

All details on a figure require subtle shading and shaping to bring the piece to life. The best source of information for faces is a mirror. Your own face is rich in color. If you were painted a straight flesh color (as many figures are, by amateurs), you would look like a Hollywood Wax Museum figure.

Look closely at the skin under the eyes; it will have a slight bluish-black tinge even if you've had plenty of sleep. The skin under the chin and in the whisker area will be darker than the rest of the face on men.

FIG. 11-1 *This entire model is built out of plastic, but the detail painting and weathering make it look like wood.*

The nose should be slightly red, as well as forehead and cheeks. This ruddy appearance is frequently attributed to sunshine, but it is actually caused by tiny blood vessels near the surface, the same ones that cause blushing.

Folds, wrinkles and clefts are usually just a shade darker than the surrounding skin because of shadows. Likewise, skin on raised areas will be just a shade lighter.

FIGURES
151

Sharpen your sense of observation and look at the colors in everything and how light plays on various surfaces. Once you've mastered this you'll be a true artist, capable of producing excellently detailed figures.

Research

Many kits come with extremely thorough directions for painting the figures or figurehead in at least one configuration. For the beginner I would advise sticking to the manufacturer's directions. As you advance, researching different costumes or uniforms can add to the enjoyment of the hobby. Researching a color scheme can even be rewarding for the novice, as it gives background information—adding a different kind of color to the project.

Any store that specializes in military miniatures will have many books on sailors of different periods. Don't worry about being able to obtain enough information; there are literally hundreds of publications available. Obviously, the more popular periods

FIG. 11–3 The Berkeley, in San Diego, houses a museum and a library which is excellent for research.

have the most books devoted to them, as well as figures. Model train shops may have figures available that are close enough to use for various scales. Companies such as Preiser or Merten have sailor figures, longshoremen, and others, in ⅟32, ⅟48, ⅟72, ⅟86, ⅟160 and ⅟220. You can be within 10 percent of scale without variations being noticeable. Besides, who's to say that a figure is 6 feet tall rather than 5 foot 8 inches?

One source of information that even professional modelers tend to overlook is their local library. Large dictionaries and encyclopedias often have several pages of color plates of the more common uniforms, flags and heralds. Even school history books are rich sources of material.

Construction

Traditionally, figures were cast in lead or white metal with a minimum of joints. There are now many companies who either build such figures in plastic for collecting or who produce figures which are coincidentally in scale to ship models.

Plastic figures are easy to assemble. The procedure is exactly like any other plastic model. File the joint areas smooth, apply a minimal amount of glue to the joint, and clamp the pieces together until set up. Sand any joint or mold release lines using #400 and #600 sandpaper respectively. Large dimples or holes can be filled with 3M Spot Putty. Follow the directions on the tube for filling or for altering the figure.

Metal figures are a little trickier to construct, but they feel more substantial when built. Other than the heft, there is really very little to recommend metal over plastic if the same figure is available both ways. Most companies recommend using epoxy or Super-Glue for assembling the figures, but both of these approaches have problems. I like using hot-melt glue. The initial cost of the gun is higher, but it can be used economically for a variety of modeling and household jobs.

Heat the figure under a bulb or in sunlight until it is just warm to the touch. Do not heat the figure much above 100 degrees, since the type of metal used has a very low melting point. Preheating will keep the glue from chilling too quickly, and will yield a stronger joint. Apply enough glue to the piece so that there will be some oozing from the seam. After 60 seconds you can trim off any excess glue flush with the surface of the figure. This glue will eliminate the need for filling the joint with body putty. Within two minutes the figure will be ready to paint.

Preparations

All of us have a certain amount of oil in our skins, which is transferred to the model while handling. This oil can cause the paint to dimple and flake off, unless the surface is prepared properly.

The two most important steps of preparation are cleaning and priming. Primer cuts through most dirts and oil and gives the surface to be painted a "tooth" for the paint to adhere to. The best type of spray primers are the automotive hot-rod gray types. These can be used on either plastic or metal. Spray on one coat lightly to just cover the surface. Any more will only be wasted effort and could hide minute detail.

DISPLAY AND STORAGE

One area rarely covered by modeling books is what to do with a model once it's complete. I've solved that problem for myself by producing dioramas in various scales as scenic display areas for my models. The displays become models in themselves and they are never really complete but rather in a state of flux. For example, I have an HO scale (1/86) wharf which is an adjunct to a model railroad layout. The fishing boat shown earlier in this book will ultimately be a part of that display. The two types of modeling work together and form an interesting display. The ship looks better in natural surroundings. Whenever I find anything odd in that scale, I add to the clutter already around the wharf.

Few people have the space they need to properly display all their models. Even most museums are hard pressed to display all their exhibits. But, like the museum curator, you can have a constantly changing display. Models can be retired to airtight plastic bags and hard boxes when not being shown.

Display base

Building a quality base for your ship can make it more attractive and improve its overall appearance.

Most arts and craft supply stores carry pre-cut blocks for bases, up to about nine inches square. The smallest blocks are great for waterline models, while the larger ones make excellent bases for a small grouping or even a small diorama.

12

FIG. 12–1 A derelict model
makes an unusual and in-
teresting display.

First, lightly sand the entire surface with #400 paper to smooth
out saw marks and to round off sharp edges.

Stain the wood with whatever color suits you and is com-
patible with the item to be displayed. A good stain is important
to the finished appearance of the display stand. I prefer Minwax,
which comes in a variety of colors. It goes on evenly and spreads
smoothly. You don't even have to wipe of excess, as with other
stains.

Allow a few hours for the stain to dry thoroughly. If any of
the wood surface raises from the moisture of the stain, sand the
surface with #600 paper. Apply a thin, even coat of semiflat (also
known as semiglossy) urethane varnish. Allow it to dry for several
hours.

FIG. 12–2 Even museum-size display cases couldn't contain every model in their collections.

After the varnish dries, remove any imperfections in the finish with very fine steel wool. It may be necessary to apply a second coat of varnish, but this would be unusual.

Simulating water

There are many different ways to simulate water. I prefer using non-odorous, non-toxic, water-based clear acrylic medium. Other modelers like epoxy resin, but I feel that method is messy, dangerous and unpredictable.

First, paint the model base with dark blue-green acrylic paint, and let it dry for several hours. Don't worry about how smooth the surface is, just keep the brush strokes going in one direction at all times.

Apply a liberal coat of clear gloss acrylic artist's medium. Let the surface become slightly tacky and add another coat. Repeat this step up until the surface looks wet and deep. Cut the model off at the waterline and position it on the base after the first couple of coats. Then, allow the acrylic to build up around the hull, especially near the bow. You can create the illusion of white caps by adding a small amount of white to the brush and lightly stroking the surface of the acrylic.

Display space

Display space is anywhere you find it. We all covet more storage or display space but few of us have the room needed (something just under that of the Smithsonian).

You can easily and inexpensively open up your house to embarassing riches of display space. You have dozens of cubic feet of display space literally lurking behind every wall. The trick is to locate and use it. The space is between sections of wallboard—that 4 inches of space between one room and another. There is approximately 14 running inches of space between studs of the standard house, which go unused except for insulation of noise. To use it, you must cut away the plasterboard or lath and plaster. But, before you attack the walls, consider the consequences. Don't cut blindly into a wall that may contain electrical conduit or foam insulation. Don't cut into an outside wall, since much of the space should be used for heat insulation. Don't cut into an area that may be needed structurally or is critical to the peace and quiet of the house. Every other wall is fair game.

The first order of business is to determine which wall would look good with a display area as a *permanent* integral part. You can't move this about once it is in place! Mistakes can be corrected with a piece of new wallboard, plaster tape and some spackle and paint, but it's work.

Next, mark off the area to be modified, if you know precisely where the studs are located. If not, buy a stud locator from a hardware store. A good size for a typical display is 14 inches wide by 10 inches high by 4 inches deep. This allows you to use stock size glass and picture frame to finish off the project.

Use a mallet to knock a hole square in the middle of the display area. Warn anyone sitting on the opposite side of the wall. Once the wall has a sizeable hole in it, probe for any obstructions with your hand, a dental mirror or a piece of coat hanger. Some

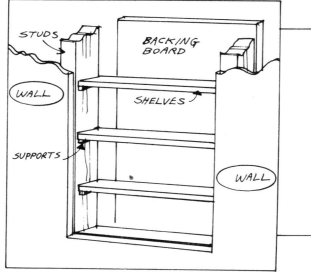

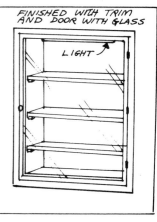

FIG. 12–3 *Display cases can be built into the unused space between wall studs.*

walls have horizontal braces which could get in the way. Avoid them if possible. Usually these are not load-bearing supports, so they can be removed without fear of the house collapsing. By the way, I hope you aren't doing this in an apartment; landlords frown on do-it-yourself demolition projects.

After you establish that the area is suitable, cut out the wall-board using a keyhole saw. You can be a little crude, because minor errors will be covered by a picture frame.

If the cuts were clean and the studs look pretty good, you can simply stain the existing wood and paint the back of the new cabinet an interesting color. Otherwise, lining the entire inside with wood will give a pleasing appearance.

Buy a picture frame and glass large enough to cover the opening and stain the wood to match the interior of the new cabinet. Shelves can be pieces of 1 × 4 pine or glass cut to fit. Glass is better if you intend to display several small models and have an interior light.

Lighting can be either fluorescent or incandescent. The latter may be easier, but the fluorescent will be more even and won't cause any heat build-up. The only problem is that the tiny lights are expensive and nearly impossible to find.

The light cord can be hidden by running it straight down behind the wall and then exiting at the baseboard. The wire can then be concealed by hiding it under the carpet or the baseboard until it reaches an outlet.

Once the models are arranged, glue a thin strip of foam to the back of the picture frame and mount the glass. Seal off any potential air leaks around the glass and especially on the inside of the case with silicone rubber. The more air-tight, the less dusting you'll have to do. Screw the picture frame to the studs in four spots and you are done! You now have storage space for models where they are free from dust and safe from little hands.

Storage

Are you familiar with the heat-sealing device for plastic bags! It is a relatively new kitchen aid which heat-seals a bag, rendering it air-tight. Most are made for only one brand of bag (the manufacturer's, of course) and have limited usefulness. General Electric makes the "Bag Sealer," which will seal any plastic bag; this is the one to get. It is the most useful modeling tool since the X-Acto knife. The ideas and applications are endless. The following are things I use mine for, but I know this isn't a complete list.

The GE unit is simple to use, but you may want to practice a little before tackling a prize job. Place the open end of the bag over the wire under the lid. Try to smooth out any wrinkles or air bubbles; make the seal as close to the object as possible. This serves to avoid waste and allows less moisture to accumulate. Never seal a moist item which can rot or rust. A little moisture in a prized catalog or on a precision tool can be disastrous. Metal items should be given a coat of WD-40 or gun oil prior to sealing. You'll be amazed at how fresh everything will stay over the years. This process is better than mummification.

The bags available in a grocery store are the most expensive. War surplus or hardware stores sell bags in hundred lots in various sizes at approximately a penny a bag. The grocery store bags are useful though, since they are thicker and can be frozen or boiled in some cases. I use the freezer bags for storing film and Krazy Glue. They can also be used for heating paint in a bottle, while minimizing the risk of the bottle breaking. Caution: do not place paints, glues, thinners or other flammable substances in boiling water. Turn off the flame and leave it off while these substances are being warmed.

The following list is a small sample of the bagger's usefulness:

1. Storing books, model catalogs, magazines, instruction sheets, etc.

2. Storing die-cast parts to prevent rust-out and paint deterioration. This also keeps rubber parts from hardening so quickly.

3. Keeping mixed bottles of paints or to extend the shelf life of glues, paints, batteries, et cetera through refrigeration.

4. Parts separation during a complicated or critical assembly. Subassemblies can be kept clean, dry, and safe.

5. Bagging and pricing items for sale at a swap-meet. You'll never lose the price and information about the model if it's bagged at home first. It also keeps models from being scratched or otherwise damaged in transit.

6. Consolidation of kits. There are many kits, or parts of kits, that I don't have the heart to discard. However, kits can soon take over a whole house. I take the kit parts and bag them with the instruction sheet. All of these bags can then be put in a large box for easy storage or hung from nails or wire from rafters.

7. Every new kit I get is opened and the chrome parts are placed in a bag and sealed immediately. These parts usually get scratched or deteriorate from the air before I get around to building the model otherwise. Most manufacturers bag the unplated plastic parts, which doesn't make a bit of sense.

8. There are many very handy, expensive tools which are invaluable when needed but often go unused for months—a small spare saw or knife blades. A quick spray with WD-40 will keep these from going bad.

9. Anyone living in L.A. knows about rubber rotting from ozone exposure. Smog, heat, and moisture can ruin rubber in no time. Coat rubber parts with silicone or WD-40 prior to bagging. You can even restore some badly hardened rubber by soaking it in Armor-All or silicone while sealed.

PHOTOGRAPHY

13. Camera equipment can be puzzling to most people, but there is no real mystery involved. Like anything else, you can learn enough about it, quickly, to enable you to enjoy photography's benefits almost immediately.

There is such a fantastic array of camera equipment to choose from that it will no doubt be confusing. However, with just a little reading of photography magazines and some common sense, you will be able to select the proper equipment for you and the job at hand.

Cameras range in price from just a few dollars for simple box cameras to over $1000 for complex professional models. Obviously, you'll most likely want something in between these two extremes.

The most popular camera on the market is known as a "single lens reflex" (you'll see it shortened to "SLR" in all photography books). This simply means that when you look through the viewfinder, you are looking directly through the lens. You see exactly what the camera lens sees.

Have you ever seen shots where everybody in the picture had their heads cut off? That's because the picture was taken with an inexpensive "range-finder" camera. It's different from a single lens reflex camera because your eye sees something quite different from what your lens "sees." The lens is mounted an inch or so lower than eye level, and is therefore looking at the scene from a different angle than you suspect.

FIG. 13–1   A 35mm single lens reflex (slr) camera is the best to use for model photography.

When you compose the picture in the viewfinder, it may look great; however, the lens is seeing the scene a bit differently. When you hit the shutter release to take the picture, you may inadvertently cut off the top half of your subject.

That won't happen with a single lens reflex camera, unless you're extremely careless. If you carefully compose the shot, you will see the same thing in the final picture. Therefore, for general purposes, an SLR is easier to use, although a bit more expensive.

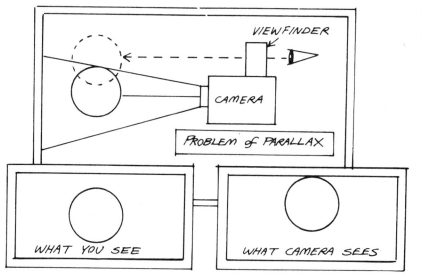

FIG. 13–2   Rangefinder cameras are ill-suited for model photography because of parallax problems.

Generally speaking, a camera is a lifetime investment, making it a good value.

Single lens reflex cameras also take a variety of accessory lenses, which make the job of photographing different subjects easier. For instance, a "wideangle" lens allows you to photograph a wider area, standing in the same spot, than you could with the standard lens. It's handy when shooting large background areas used as backdrop for your main subject, and it has good depth of field for image sharpness.

If you want to shoot a photo of something that is quite far away, attach a telephoto lens (sometimes called a "long" lens). This, very simply, brings in far-away subjects to fill up the picture with your subject.

FIG. 13–3 *Backlighting can completely wash out the subject.*

Those three lenses will cover almost every situation you are liable to encounter. In addition, you'll need film, common sense, a talk with your local camera store operator, and practice.

Most SLR cameras accept 35mm film. It's very inexpensive, so shoot a lot of it. Buy 36-exposure rolls, so you avoid reloading all the time. I highly recommend Kodak Tri-X black and white film. It's an excellent film that allows you to practically shoot in the dark without a flash.

The Japanese have brought 35mm photography within nearly everyone's grasp with their mass-produced, high-quality cameras. Go to your camera store and have a salesman help you. Pick up the cameras, handle them, ask questions. Many have interchangeable lenses, and they will usually feature a through the-lens light meter which allows correct exposure of the film according to how

FIG. 13–4 Photos with extreme light-dark contrasts are very difficult; the light areas will wash out, while the dark turn into almost solid black blobs.

FIG. 13–5 The people in this photo were deliberately blurred so as not to detract from the model in the foreground.

much light is available. Since each camera operates a bit differently, you will have to familiarize yourself with the camera you purchase. Read the instruction manual over and over, and handle the camera (without film in it) before you attempt a picture-taking session.

Processing

If you've shot, say, five rolls of 36-exposure film, that's 180 shots! Obviously you can't afford to have a print made of each one, even at cut-rate drugstore prices, let alone at a custom printer. Instead, take the film to a camera shop and tell them that you want the film developed and a proof or contact sheet made of each roll.

A proof sheet contains a very small black and white print of each shot. Each print is actually the same size as each frame of the film. These sheets are used by professional photographers to

FIG. 13–6   A proof sheet will help you pick the best shots without going to the expense of having prints made of all the shots you take.

pick out only the best shots. Since all the shots you take won't be sensational photos, why pay to have prints made of bad, or uninteresting, shots? Use the proof sheet to pick out only the very best.

The biggest problem when photographing miniatures is usually depth of field. Consider this: a real ship is sailing in front of mountains on a bright day. With a standard lens (wide-angle or normal lens) you should be able to capture the ship, mountains and sky all in focus. In order to recreate this in miniature, special precautions must be taken to get proper depth. A limited depth of field always destroys the illusion of reality. The closer the miniature to the camera, the less depth of field, so keep your distance. Wide-angle lenses have more apparent sharpness than telephoto lenses. Large F-stop (F/22 or 32)/small aperture offers more depth of field than a small F-stop (F/1.8)/large aperture.

GLOSSARY OF NAUTICAL TERMS

ABAFT. Toward the rear of the ship, behind.

ABEAM. Across the ship, from side to side.

ABOVE. Higher point on ship, above deck.

AFT. See abaft.

AFTER. See abaft.

AFTERBODY. The ship's hull aft of midships.

AHEAD. Forward, towards the front.

ALOFT. Above, in the rigging.

ANCHOR. Secures ship to sea floor, fish-hook-shaped.

ANCHOR BILL. See Bill.

ANCHOR CABLE. Cable or chain which secures anchor to ship.

ANCHOR, FISHED. Anchor secured at ship's side.

ANCHOR RING. Secures anchor to cable.

ANCHOR STOCK. Wooden cross-bar on anchor.

ANVIL. Used for shaping metal.

ARM. A yard, a yard arm, 3 feet from nose to fingertip.

ASTERN. Behind the ship.

ATHWART. Across the ship from side to side.

ATHWARTSHIP. Located side for side across ship.

BACK. To back an anchor with a smaller one to ease strain.

BACK ROPE. Jib boom supporting line.

BACK STAY. Mast supporting line aft of the shrouds.

BARE POLES. Ship with sails furled.

BARK. Three-masted square rigger.

BASE LINE. Reference point for any dimensional data on blueprints.

FIG. G–1   Various levels of a ship.

BATTEN.   Wood strip used as a fastener, as in "Batten down (secure) the hatches."

BEAK HEAD.   The farthest point forward on the bow.

BEAT.   To sail as directly into the wind as possible.

BEAM.   The width of the ship at its widest point.

BEATING.   Going toward the wind, as in tacking.

BECALM.   To intercept the wind.

BECKET.   Connecting link on the bottom of a block.

BED.   Adjustable platform for guns.

BEE BLOCK.   A secured block with holes for leading lines.

BEE HOLES.   Holes used for leading lines.

BEFORE THE WIND.   Sailing with the wind at your back.

BELAY.   To tie off a line (see belaying pin).

BELAYING PIN.   A turned rod that fits in the pin rail to secure lines.

BELOW.   Below decks.

BEND.   To fasten.

BILL.   The tips of an anchor which look like bird bills.

BILLBOARD.   Reinforced area of hull where anchor rests.

BINNACLE.   Mounting case for compass.

BIGHT.   The loop in a rope doubled over.

BILGE.   The lowest part of the ship besides keel.

BITTS.   Vertical posts used in securing lines.

BLACKWALL HITCH.   A knot used to tie a line to a hook.

BLOCK.   See Pulley.

BOB STAY.   The part of the bowsprit rigging which starts at the end of the bowsprit and ends at the waterline.

BOLSTER.   To reinforce. Also a piece of wood used on another piece to ease chafing.

BOLSTRO.   Outer edge of sail to which canvas is sewn.

BOLT.   A rope used to edge a sail, giving it more strength.

BONNET.   An extra section of sail added to a square sail.

BOOM.   A pole used to spread sails.

BOOM JAWS.   A U-shaped pivot on the base of a boom.

BOW.   The front of a ship.

BOWLINE.   A knot; or, a line used for hauling a sail forward.

BOWSPRIT.   The jutting pole at the bow.

BRACE.   A line for hauling yards.

BRAIL.   See Buntline.

BREECHING.   A line attached to a cannon to control recoil.

BRIDLES.   Lines used to spread a load over a greater distance.

BRIG.   An area used for detention, a jail; or, a two-masted square rigger.

BRIGANTINE.   See Brig, second definition.

BROACH TO.   To swing a vessel running before the wind.

BULKHEAD.   An internal wall of a ship.

BULLOCK BLOCKS.   A two-sheaved block.

BULWARKS.   Upper sides between deck and rail.

BUMPKIN.   Short projection at side of ship for rigging.

BUNT.   The middle of a sail.

BUNTLINE.   Line at lower edge of sail used for furling.

BUTT.   The end of a plank where it mates up to another plank. A (scuttle) butt is used for holding drinking water.

BUTTOCKS.   Rear of ship.

CABLE.   Heavy line of rope or steel.

CAMBER.   The side to side curve of the deck.

CANT FRAME.   A frame not perpendicular to the keel.

CAP RAIL.   Top railing on deck.

CAPSTAN.   A vertical winch used for hauling lines.

CAPSTAN BAR.   Lever used for turning capstan.

CASCABEL.   Knob at rear of gun.

CASTLE.   Structure above main deck.

CATHARPINS.   Rigging running transversely to connect futtock shroud ends.

CATHEAD.   Forward projection to which anchor is first hoisted.

CAULKING.   Hemp (rope) soaked in tar to seal against water.

CAVIL.   A two-pronged rod for tying off lines on a rail.

CEILING.   Inboard planking.

CHAIN PIPE.   Hole in the ship's side for anchor chain.

CHAIN PLATE.   Metal link connecting lower end of shroud with ship side.

CHAIN SPAN.   A chain portion of a halliard between the tie, the ship side, and the halliard tackle.

CHANNEL.   "Chain Wales"—Narrow platforms on the ship side into which lower ends of shrouds are connected.

CHASE.   Main barrel of gun.

CHEEK.   1) Of mast: reinforcement block on mast side under trestle

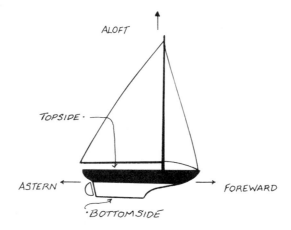

tree. 2) Of bow: curved reinforcement timber between fore part of the ship and the stern.

CHOCK.   Wooden block used as a stopper.

CLAMP STRAKE.   The first ceiling plank under a deck beam.

CLEAT.   T-shaped fitting for fastening a line.

CLEW.   1) The corner of a sail; the hole in the sail through which rigging is rove. 2) Clew line: line that hauls the lower outboard corner of a sail up to its yard.

CLEW GARNET.   The clew line of a lower sail (main or fore course).

CLOSE HAULED.   Sails pulled as close to parallel with the keel as possible.

CLOVE HITCH.   Knot.

COME ABOUT.   Change a ship's tack by sailing first into the wind.

COMPANIONWAY.   Access door and stairs.

COMPASS.   Navigational device that indicates ship's direction with respect to the North pole.

COURSE.   1) A ship's direction. 2) A lower sail, e.g. main course, fore course.

CRANSE IRONS.   Metal fittings for pivoting a yard to a mast.

CROSSJACK.   Lowest yard on the mizzen mast.

CROSS TREES.   1) Transverse bars at the top of a mast. 2) The structure at the topmast doublings.

CROWN OF ANCHOR.   End of anchor shank opposite the ring.

CROW'S FOOT.   A web of rigging usually set up to prevent sails from chafing against other gear.

DAVIT.   Crane support for a boat.

DEAD BLOCK.   Block with holes for leading lines.

DEAD EYE. Wooden disc with three holes, used in setting up elements of standing rigging.

DEADWOOD. Portion of a ship's keel structure outboard of her body frames.

DECK. On land, the floor. A horizontal surface of the ship's structure.

DECK BEAM. Transverse timber that supports a deck.

DECK HOUSE. A shelter built on an upper deck.

DISTANCE LINE. A rigging line whose function is to keep equal spacing between a number of elements, e.g. the sail hoops on a gaffsail.

DOLPHIN. A lifting ring on a gun.

DOLPHIN STRIKER. A short spar projecting downward from the end of a bowsprit.

DOUBLINGS. Portion of mast structure where an upper and lower mast overlap.

DOWN HAUL. Line for pulling down a sail or yard.

DOWN WIND. In the direction the wind is blowing.

DRUM, WHEEL. Part of rigging connecting the steering wheel with the tiller.

EARRING. Connecting devices between the upper corners of a sail and the yardarm.

EASE OFF. To steer a ship more down wind.

EKING. Longitudinal reinforcing timbers in the deck framing.

EYE BOLT. Rigging attachment.

EYE SPLICE. Loop in end of rope formed by splicing.

FAIR LEAD. A guide for ropes and lines.

FALL OFF. Steer more down wind.

FID. Wooden block that works as a stopper, e.g. the top mast fid stops the heel of the topmast on the trestle trees.

FIDDLE BLOCK. Two-sheaved block where the sheaves are mounted one on top of the other.

FIFE RAIL. Pin rail mounted at foot of mast.

FIGUREHEAD. Decorative carving on a ship's forepeak.

FISHING TACKLE, ANCHOR. Tackle for hauling fluke end of anchor up to the ship side or rail.

FLEMISH HORSE. Small extra foot rope on outermost end of yard.

FLUKE OF ANCHOR. Spade-like end of an anchor arm.

FLYING JIB. One of several sails set on the head spars and fore rigging.

FOOT OF SAIL. The lower edge of a sail.

FOOT ROPE. Rigged under a spar to support sailors at work.

FORE. The front of the ship.

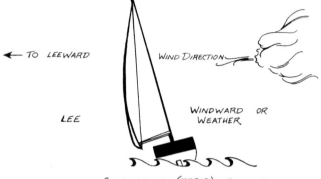

TO LEEWARD

WIND DIRECTION

WINDWARD OR WEATHER

LEE

SHIP LEANS (HEELS) TO LEEWARD

FORECASTLE, FO'C'SLE. 1) Forward structure and deck above the main deck. 2) The crew's living quarters.

FORE CHAINS. Link attachment of a fore shroud to the ship side.

FORE CHANNEL. See Channel.

FORE DECK. Deck of the forecastle.

FOREMAST. Foremost lower mast.

FORE PEAK. Structure at the foremost part of the bows, e.g. head rails, gratings, cheek knees.

FORE TACK. See Tack.

FORWARD. Toward the front of the ship.

FRAME. Structure that forms one of the ship's body sections.

FULL OFF. Sailing straight down wind.

FULL-RIGGED SHIP. Three-masted square rigger.

FURL. To roll up and store sails.

FUTTOCK SHROUD. Extensions of upper mast shrouds leading downward from the ends of the cross trees and in toward a point on the lower mast.

FURNITURE. General term for the fittings and gear fastened to a ship's deck.

GAFF. Spar that spreads the top edge of a gaff sail.

GAFF SAIL. Fore and aft, four-sided sail.

GALLERY, QUARTER GALLERY, STERN GALLERY. Narrow cabin built out on the side or stern of a vessel.

GAMMONING. Stout lashing tying the bowsprit down to the stern.

GILL GUY. A flexible fairlead attached to a shroud or stay.

GRAPNEL. A four-pronged anchor.

GRATING. Grill-like decking.

GRIPES. Lashings for lifeboats.

GROUND TACKLE.   Anchoring equipment.

GUDGEON.   Female portion of rudder mounting.

GUM.   Artillery.

GUN DECK.   Main deck.

GUN PORT.   Opening in the side of a ship through which gun was fired.

GUN TACKLE.   A 1-to-1 tackle.

GUY.   Supplementary standing rigging line, e.g. whisker boom guy.

HALLIARD.   Line for hauling up a sail.

HALL'S ANCHOR.   Anchor with pivoted flukes.

HATCH.   Opening in a deck for access to lower areas.

HAWSE PIPE.   See Chain pipe.

HAWSERS.   Heavy, cable-laid line used as anchor cable.

HEAD.   1) The bow. 2) The ship's latrine.

HEAD NETTINGS.   Nets rigged under the bowsprit to catch head sails as they are brought down.

HEAD RAILS.   Curved rails from under the catheads up to the forepeak.

HEAD SAIL.   Any one of the sails set on the bowsprit and its extensions.

HEAD UP.   To steer the ship into the wind.

HEART.   A hardwood, triangular shaped donut used in setting up heavy standing rigging.

HEAVE TO.   To bring the ship to a stop by heading her into the wind.

HEEL.   1) The lean of a ship to leeward. 2) The bottom of a mast.

HELM.   Ship's steering apparatus.

HELMSMAN.   A ship's steersman.

HERMAPHRODITE BRIG.   See Brigantine.

HITCH.   A general class of knots.

HULL.   The main body of a ship exclusive of masts, rigging and deck furniture.

INBOARD.   Toward the centerline of the ship; within the shipsides.

IN HAUL.   Line for pulling a sail in—see down haul.

IRON.   General term for metal fittings on spars.

JACK STAY.   Rod mounted on yard to which sail was bent.

JEER.   Heavy tackle for lifting a lower yard into place.

JIB.   Head sail set on the jib boom.

JIB BOOM.   Spar extension of the bow sprit.

JIB-OF-JIB BOOM.   Spar extension of the jib boom.

JOGGLE PLANK.   Element of hull planking.

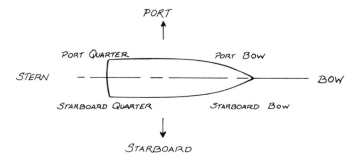

FIG. G–4 Directional references as viewed from navigator's viewpoint facing forward (bow).

KEEL.   The bottom, central timber a ship's hull.

KEELSON.   An inboard central timber running parallel and above the keel and above the body frames.

KETCH.   Two-masted fore and aft rigged ship in which the foremast is the taller of the two.

KEVEL.   See Cavil.

KNEE.   Corner braces in a ship's framework.

KNIGHT HEAD.   Heavy vertical timbers in the bows for tying off lines.

LADDER.   Ship's stairs or steps.

LANYARD.   1) Light line used to lace together pairs of deadeyes, hearts, et cetera, on shrouds and stays. 2) Any short length of rope used as a handle or trigger.

LASHING.   A wrapping of rope tying two or more elements together.

LEE.   The downwind side of a ship.

LEE HELM.   A helm that requires steering pressure to keep the ship from heading up into the wind.

LEECH.   The outer edge of a square sail; the after edge of a fore and aft sail.

LEEWARD.   In the direction the wind is blowing.

LIFEBOAT.   Auxiliary emergency craft.

LIFT.   Line for tilting yard up and down.

LUBBER'S HOLE.   Access hole in mast top structure.

LUFF.   Forward edge of a fore and aft sail.

LUFF TACKLE.   2-to-1 tackle.

MAIN MAST.   Principal and largest mast of a vessel.

MAIN WALE.   Major longitudinal structural member on the side of the ship.

MARLIN.   Tarred twine used for whipping and serving.

MARTINGALE. Jib boom rigging line that holds jib boom down and aft.

MAST. Vertical pole that supports sails and other gear.

MAST CAP. Structural component at limit of mast's height.

MAST CHEEK. See Cheek.

MAST COAT. Fitting around mast at level of deck.

MAST PARTNER. Deck reinforcements around a mast hole.

MAST STEP. Structure in the ship for holding the heel of a lower mast.

MAST HEAD. Vicinity of the top of a mast.

MESSENGER LINE. Long loop used to heave up anchor.

MIDSHIPS. Center section of ship.

MIZZEN. Aftermost mast of a fully rigged ship.

MOON SAIL, MOONRAKER. Sail and rigging above the skysail.

MOUSE. Knotwork padding around upper end of lower stay; formed stopper for eye end of stay.

PAD EYE. Metal eye fastened to a plate bolted to the deck.

PAINTER. Towing line for a boat.

PARREL. Bearing device between a spar and mast.

PARTNER. See Mast partner.

PAWL. Stop cleat for a windlass ratchet.

PEAK. Top of a fore and aft sail.

PEAK HALLIARD. Halliard for the high corner of a gaff sail.

PENDANT. A component of certain tackles.

PIN RAIL. Special rail fitted to bulwark and drilled for belaying pins.

PINTLE. Male component of rudder mounting.

POOP DECK. A short deck above the quarter deck, usually clear aft.

POOP LANTERN, STERN LANTERN. Large, horn-lensed lanterns that hung over the stern of 17th-century ships.

PORT. Left.

PORT HOLE. Round ship window.

PUT ABOUT. Come about.

QUADRANT. Large, modern tiller worked by engines.

QUARTER. Sides of a ship aft.

QUARTER DECK. Partial deck aft above the main deck.

QUARTER GALLERY. See Gallery.

QUOIN. Wedge for adjusting gun elevation.

RATLINE. Rope ladder hung in shrouds.

REACH. To sail with the wind coming from the side.

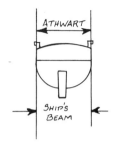

FIG. G–5   Hull reference points.

REEF.   To reduce the area of a sail by tying a section up against a spar.

REEF BAND.   A reinforced strip across a sail through which the reef lines are rove.

REEF KNOT.   Square knot.

REEVE.   To fit or lead a rigging line through a sheave fair lead.

RIDING BITTS.   Heavy timber structure to which the anchor cable is tied.

RIGGING.   General term for rope and cable and associated equipment.

RING BOLT.   An eye bolt with a ring fixed into its eye.

ROBAND, RIBBAND.   Line for lacing a sail to a spar.

ROLLING HITCH.   Knot.

ROPE WALK.   Rope-making apparatus.

ROVE TO ADVANTAGE.   A tackle configuration where the hauling end emerges from the block nearest the load.

ROYAL MAST.   Sail and rigging above the top gallant mast.

RUDDER.   Vertical steering panel hinged to the stern post.

RUDDER POST, RUDDER STOCK.   Extension from the top of the rudder to which the tiller is attached.

RUN BEFORE THE WIND.   Sail with the wind.

RUNNER.   Tackle configuration with but one single-sheaved block.

RUNNING LIGHT.   Light to indicate ship's location.

RUNNING RIGGING.   Operational rigging.

SCARF, SCARF JOINT.   Method of joining two lengths of planking.

SCHOONER.   Fore and aft rigged ship with two or more masts.

SHACKLE.   U-shaped metal link with a pin fitted to the open end for connecting lines, and chain.

SHANK OF ANCHOR.   Central vertical bar of anchor.

SHEAVE.   Grooved wheel mounted in a block or elsewhere for leading lines around corners.

SHEER POLE.   Wooden rung mounted on the shrouds just above the deadeyes.

SHEET.   Line that hauls lower outboard corner of a sail aft.

SHEET BEND.   Knot.

SHROUD.   Element of standing rigging which leads aft to the ship side from the mast top.

SISTER HOOK.   A pair of hooks which overlap to become a closed ring.

SKYLIGHT.   Deck structure with windows to admit light below.

SKYSAIL.   Mast and rigging above the royal mast.

SLING.   Rigging component that holds a yard to the mast at the pivot point.

SLOOP.   Single-masted vessel.

SNATCH BLOCK.   Block with an open, hook-like shell.

SPACER LINE.   See Distance line.

SPANKER.   After-most gaff sail on a square rigger.

SPAR.   General term for a ship's poles.

SPLICE.   Rope or cable joint formed by interweaving of the strands.

SPRING STAY.   One of the upper mast stays.

SPRITSAIL.   Square sail set under the bowsprit, 17th–18th century.

SPRIT TOP SAIL.   Small square sail set on a short mast (sprit top-mast) mounted on the end of the bowsprit, 17th century.

STANDING RIGGING.   Permanently set up rigging whose function is the support of the spars.

STARBOARD, "STEER BOARD."   The right side of the ship; to the right.

STAY.   A line of standing rigging that runs from near the top of a mast to a point forward and lower on the ship.

STAYSAIL.   Sail set on a stay.

STEALER.   Element of hull planking.

STEM.   Foremost vertical timber in the bow.

STERN.   After part of a ship.

STERN POST.   Aftermost vertical timber.

STIRRUP.   Hanging support line for a footrope.

STRAKE.   Plank of a ship's hull.

STRINGER.   Longitudinal member of hull structure.

STROP.   Block fastening.

STUDDING SAIL, STUNSAIL.   Light auxiliary sail set outboard of the end of a yard on a boom.

TACK.   1) Referring to the side of the ship against which the wind is blowing, e.g. starboard track, port tack. 2) Line for hauling the lower outboard corner of lower sail forward.

TACKLE.   System of rope and blocks to increase leverage on a line.

TAFFRAIL.   Above-water stern panel.

THIMBLE.   Reinforcement for a sail cringle or loop of a line.

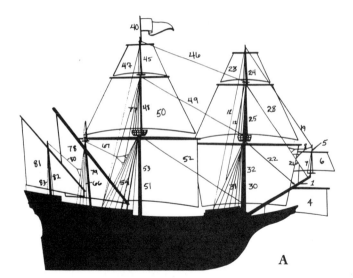

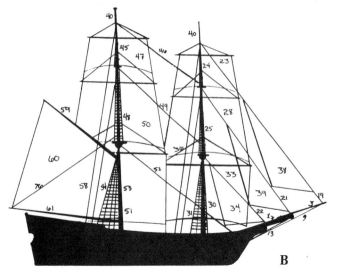

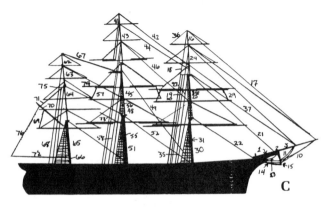

FIG. G–6   Rigging glossary of terms.

1. BOWSPRIT   A, B, C
2. BOWSPRIT CAP   C
3. JIBBOOM   B, C
4. SPRITSAIL   A
5. SPRIT TOP MAST   A
6. SPRIT TOP SAIL   A
7. SPRIT TOPMAST SHROUDS   A
8. SPRIT TOPMAST BACKSTAY   A
9. SINGLE MARTINGALE   B
10. OUTER MARTINGALE   C
11. INNER MARTINGALE   C
12. BACKSTAY   A
13. BOBSTAY   B, C
14. BACKROPE   C
15. DOLPHIN STRIKER   C
16. FORE ROYAL MAST   C
17. FORE ROYAL STAY   C
18. FORE ROYAL BACK STAY   C
19. FORE TOPGALLANT STAY   A, B, C
20. FORE TOPGALLANT BACKSTAY   C
21. FORE TOPMAST STAY   A, B, C
22. FORE STAY   A, B, C
23. FORE TOPGALLANT SAIL   A, B
24. FORE TOPGALLANT MAST   A, B, C
25. FORE TOPMAST   A, B, C
26. FORE TOPMAST SHROUDS   C
27. FORE TOPMAST BACKSTAYS   C
28. FORE TOPSAIL   A, B
29. FORE TOPSAIL SHEET   C
30. FOREMAST   A, B, C
31. FORE SHROUDS   A, B, C
32. FORE COURSE   A
33. FORE SAIL   B
34. FORE STAY SAIL   B
35. FORE BACKSTAY   C
36. LIFT   B, C
37. JIB STAY   C
38. OUTER JIB   B
39. INNER JIB   B
40. FLAGSTAFF   A, B
41. SKYSAIL MAST   C
42. SKY SAIL STAY   C
43. MAIN ROYAL MAST   C
44. MAIN ROYAL STAY   C
45. MAIN TOPGALLANT MAST   A, B, C
46. MAIN TOP GALLANT STAY   A, B, C
47. MAIN TOP GALLANT SAIL   A, B
48. MAIN TOPMAST   A, B, C
49. MAIN TOPMAST STAY   A, B, C
50. MAIN TOP SAIL   A, B
51. MAIN MAST   A, B, C
52. MAIN STAY   A, B, C
53. MAIN COURSE   A, B
54. MAIN SHROUDS   A, B
55. MAIN LOWER MAST SHROUDS   C
56. MAIN TOPMAST SHROUDS   C
57. MAIN UPPER TOPSAIL SHEET   C
58. MAIN BACKSTAYS   B, C
59. MAIN GAFF   B
60. MAIN GAFF SAIL   B
61. MAIN BOOM   B
62. MIZZEN ROYAL MAST   C
63. MIZZEN TOPGALLANT MAST   C
64. MIZZEN TOP MAST   C
65. MIZZEN MAST   C
66. MIZZEN SHROUDS   A, C
67. MIZZEN STAYS   A, C
68. MIZZEN BACK STAYS   A, C
69. MIZZEN UPPER TOPSAIL SHEET   C
70. SPANKER GAFF   C
71. SPANKER GAFF TOPPING LIFT   C
72. SPANKER BOOM   C
73. SPENCER GAFF   C
74. STUN SAIL BOOM   C
75. SWIFTERS   C
76. TOPPING LIFT   B, C
77. FUTLOCK SHROUDS   A
78. LATEEN MIZZEN SAIL   A
79. LATTEEN MIZZEN MAST   A
80. BONVENTURE MIZZEN STAY   A
81. BONVENTURE MIZZEN SAIL   A
82. BONVENTURE MIZZEN MAST   A
83. BONVENTURE MIZZEN SHROUDS   A

THOLE PINS.   Pins mounted in the gunwale of a rowboat as lever points for the oars.

THWART.   Transverse framing member of a boat.

TIE.   Element of a halliard or jeers.

TILLER.   Steering bar from the top of the rudder.

TIMBER.   General term for ship's structural components.

TIMBERHEAD.   Upper, exposed end of body frame.

TIMBER HITCH.   Knot.

TOP.   Platform structure near the top of a lower mast.

TOPGALLANT.   Mast sail and rigging above the topmast.

TOPMAST.   Sail and rigging above the lower mast.

TOPSIDE.   Above deck.

TOUCH HOLE.   Hole in cannon for holding firing primer.

TRAILBOARD.   Carved, decorated stem reinforcement panel.

TRANSOM.   Stern panel above water, also taffrail.

TRESTLE TREES.   Fore and aft structural members of a mast top.

TRUCK.   Ball or cap at the top limit of the highest mast in a mast structure

TRUNNEL, TRENNEL.   "Tree Nail," wooden dowel used to fasten a plank to a frame.

TRUNNION.   Support bar on a gun.

TRUSS.   Lashing to hold a yard to a mast at the pivot point.

TUB PARREL.   Metal parrel, 19th century.

TURNBUCKLE.   Metal linking device with screw adjustments for varying tension on a line.

WALE.   Longitudinal structural member of a ship's side.

WATER LINE.   1) Line that designates the hull shape on a plane parallel with that of the water. 2) Line between the above and below water parts of a ship's hull.

WATERWAY.   Outermost deck plank.

WEAR.   To change a square rigger's tack by sailing first downwind.

WEATHER.   The direction from which the wind blows.

WEATHER SIDE.   The side of the ship against which the wind is blowing.

WEATHER HELM.   A helm that requires steering pressure to keep the ship from sailing down wind. Also see Lee helm.

WHEEL BOX.   Structure for housing steering gear.

WHELP.   Shallow triangular rib on the barrel of a capstan or windlass.

WHIPPING.   A wrapping of twine on the end of a rope.

WHIPSTAFF.   Early steering lever.

WHISKER BOOM.   Short spar descending laterally from the side of the bowsprit.

WINDING TACKLE.   3-to-2 tackle.

WINDLASS.   Hauling engine with a horizontal barrel mounted between two uprights.

WINDWARD.   The direction from which the wind is blowing.

WOOLDING.   Metal or rope reinforcement wrappings around a mast.

YARD, YARDARM.   Transverse spar on a square rigger.

YAWL.   Two-masted vessel with a small after mast stepped usually aft of the rudder post.

YOKE.   Structural component of a yard where it fits to the mast.

INDEX

Page numbers in **bold** refer to information in illustrations